A WRITER'S
SURVIVAL GUIDE
TO GETTING PUBLISHED

TERRY W. BURNS

Port
Yonder
Press

Since 2009

A Writer's Survival Guide To Getting Published

Copyright © 2010 Terry Burns

A Writer's Survival Guide to Getting Published
Port Yonder Books (a division of Port Yonder Press, LLC)
www.PortYonderPress.com

ISBN 978-1-935600-03-9
Library of Congress Control Number: 2010934808

Editorial team: Linda Yezak, Naomi Musch, Chila "Maggie" Woychik,
Kristine Pratt, Lisa Lickel
Book cover and interior design by Anna O'Brien, behindthegift.com
Logo design by Tony Lavoie

Available direct from your local bookstore, online, or
from the publisher at: www.PortYonderPress.com
For more info on the author and this book visit:
www.terryburns.net.books.aspx

Printed in the United States of America.

☙ DEDICATION ❧

This book is dedicated to the many
ACFW *(American Christian Fiction Writers)*
members who participated in the online course and
helped formulate this material.

ENDORSEMENTS
Course Comments

[Terry Burns] removed a great deal of confusion and fear from the process required for the writer to be recognized by an agent or an editor. He discussed everything from the proposal cover letter to the "dreaded" synopsis and all that "scary" stuff that lies in between. It's not an easy process, but nothing worth having ever is.

Patti Shene

My highest compliments on the job you did in presenting this material. I found it practical, honest, insightful, and clear. You offer a lot of wisdom in what you've presented. I see this as excellent material for a person just starting out, and reassuring for someone who is farther down the writing path.

Max Elliot Anderson

This was a tremendously helpful course. I so appreciate your time and effort to respond to all our questions, even in the midst of recovering from an injury! Although I didn't participate much, I was inspired to get off my duff and put on my "I am a writer" hat by putting together a website and blog. It seems every day I had a question answered I hadn't even thought to ask. Your explanation about why agents and editors want to see a synopsis changed my whole perspective on the dreaded thing! What a blessing you've been to us all, thank you so much!

Niki Turner

I ended up mostly lurking but I learned so much. I learned that I can hide behind my "VP on Stage" persona and not be as afraid to pitch (I hope!). I so appreciate all the time you took, and for giving a thorough class with such useable material. Thank you seems rather puny by comparison.

Pamela James

OK, maybe it's just me, but I think calling what you sent us "this little eBook" is just slightly understated. Or maybe WAY understated. The online classes are always great, but I learned more this month than I ever expected. You've created a resource that I hope many writers learn about and use. I know I'll be saving this to my hard drive and coming back to it again and again. I believe that this is the best ACFW online course I've taken. Terry was very personable and willing to answer all of our silly and serious questions.

Leigh DeLozier

As I already told him, in my opinion this course all by itself was worth my ACFW membership dues. It was so very helpful and practical. I can't thank Terry enough for all the hard work he put into it.

LeAnn Austin

Terry was fantastic as an instructor. I think everyone would give an overwhelmingly positive response to his teaching style/method and his content. I just couldn't say enough wonderful things about what he shared with us!!

Judythe Morgan

Thank you so much for taking the time to answer all our endless questions with such patience. Not everyone would be so selfless. Hope to meet you someday and thank you in person.

Darlo Gemeinhardt

Thank you, Terry, for breaking this elephantine task down into bite-size chunks. You've given me the courage and the tools to pursue my longest-standing dream. God bless you!

Kathleen L. Maher

I'm ready to start a Terry Burns fan club! What a generous, kind, thoughtful man!

Modestly Unsigned

NOTE

This book is derived from an on-line course,
"How to Pitch and Promote Like a Pro," presented to ACFW members.
Questions and individual comments are italicized in the book.

TABLE OF CONTENTS

CHAPTER ONE

OVERCOMING SHYNESS

Hello, my name is Terry Burns,
and I'm too shy to pitch
and promote.

Yes, I've always been very shy. I used to be the kid who stood over on the side of the playground watching the other kids play. When in high school, I was so shy the lady who is now my wife had to invite me out. I don't order pizza, I don't take things back to the store, and if you serve me a bad meal in a restaurant, I won't complain. I just won't come back.

When I got to college, I was required to take a speech course for a business degree. I told the teacher I would never stand up in front of the class and talk, even if he failed me. He responded by teaching me how to invent a public persona and hide behind it. He changed my life.

That's how we're going to start.

If life were fair, we could stay home and write our books. Then, when we got one completed, we could burn a piece of special paper in the fireplace (the way they do in Rome when a Pope is elected), and publishers would line up at our door four abreast fighting for the chance to offer us an obscene amount of money for our brainchild. They would carry our precious manuscript off and do everything necessary beyond that point to turn it into a best seller, while we worked on our next masterpiece.

If anyone truly believes that, I'm sorry to have to be the one to break the news to them. It's not going to happen. And we might as well talk about the tooth fairy and the Easter bunny while we're at it.

The truth is, if we want to be successful novelists but are totally unwilling or unable to pitch and promote, there is little need for us to continue writing. The odds of success are such a long-shot without pitching and promoting, that writing is a waste of time.

Whew, those are hard words.

A number of years ago, I was about to talk at a conference and was visiting with a couple dozen writers in a hospitality room the night before. They kept saying things like: "I could never stand up in front of a group like that," or, "There's no way I could sit down and pitch to an editor." Another: "I can get up and talk in front of ten, fifty, or a hundred people, but don't ask me to meet with someone I don't know well in a one-on-one situation."

There were many other such comments that showed me they were part of the "too shy" club. I realized I was planning to talk about the wrong thing, and the next day *How to Pitch and Promote Like a Pro* was born.

There is a whole scale, from "just a little bit shy" to "absolute recluse," involved in being a shy person. I'm pretty far up the scale, but as the speech instructor pointed out, so was Johnny Carson.

What?

Yes, I'm told Carson was so shy that he could hardly converse with those in the backstage crew — until he walked out on that stage, put his hands behind his back, puffed out his chest, and turned into the consummate entertainer.

This is a very common trait with writers. Many of us are drawn to expressing ourselves in writing since it is so difficult for us to communicate verbally.

In order for me to teach that first course I had to admit my problem to the group, the Ozark Writers League (OWL) to be exact, and it was something I had never done. I had some good friends at that meeting who had known me for years, and they didn't believe I was telling the truth. They didn't believe it because I tend to only meet writing friends in writing groups, which means I'm in character when I'm there, and I simply do not appear to be shy when I'm in character. Now that they know, they can see me standing over at the side of the room quietly watching everyone, and they know I am out of character. I become the kid on the edge of the playground again.

Some people like me never get over being shy and just learn how to deal with it. Some actually change. We have both sides in our nature, and it is merely a process of learning how to bring the other side out. Some just learn a few tips on how to change their position on that shyness scale to the degree they want.

    I don't believe you're really that shy.

Believe it.

I was a Chamber of Commerce executive for twenty-seven years. How's that for a vocational choice for someone with my social disability? But once I learned how to get into character and use it, I went straight at my problem and took it on. Chamber people have a lot of meetings of all kinds, and some can even be quite adversarial.

I was terrified at my first one, and believe me that is not an understatement. But God took a hand.

There was a group of men who liked to sing barbershop. Of the quartet, three were standing over to the side singing a little as they had done for many years, but one was missing. I sang a little barbershop in college (another major stretch for me), and without thinking stepped in and started filling in the missing tenor part. From that point on, I had three of the most powerful Chamber executives in the state as my protectors and guides, and had a wonderful time at the conference.

Most of this part of the book will be spent showing you that developing a personal persona is possible and getting you convinced you can do it. If you just read what I've written so far and think, "If he can do it, I can do it," this part of the text might be over for you right now. But I know from experience, and from doing this gig somewhere around a hundred times or so, that the hardest person to sell on this concept is you, not the people you want to convince.

One person asked: As Christian authors, doesn't this mean we are being false?
Another: How do we find the confidence to pitch and promote without losing all humility?

We all have both outgoing and retiring sides to our personalities. We're just talking about some ways we can bring out a different side of our personality. Like you, I am a totally different person when I am in character than when I am being myself. But they are both me. People who are only a little shy can do this with much less effort. Those of us who are terribly shy have to make a long stretch between the two.

Actually, this is something all of us do naturally. We project different personas in different areas of our lives. A woman is different in her role as mother than she is on the job. She's different at church than when she's being a soccer mom. And dad is certainly different as a father than he is on the job, or in the locker room. Generally, we adopt this persona naturally. If we have trouble in one of our daily roles maybe it's actually because we just shifted naturally and didn't give much thought to how we wanted to project ourselves.

Here we actually have a chance to design the persona we wish to project to accomplish what we need to accomplish. And yes, in extreme situations, we can actually project it and hide behind it.

Shyness manifests itself in different ways. One lady said she would rather talk in person than on an impersonal computer. Many others say just the opposite. Some can talk to a group but not one on one, and again others are just the opposite. Some are only shy when they get into certain situations.

The common ingredient to all of these is comfort level. For some reason, some things are comfortable for people to do and other things aren't. We're going to talk about how to increase that comfort level.

A few years ago, I read a booklet by Joyce Meyer: "Do It Afraid." It has become my motto. I can go into a room and make you think I know everything about everyone while I try to keep my heart from beating out of my chest. Each time it gets a little bit easier, especially as I learn about a topic/situation. The more I know, the more comfortable I am.

Most people who have met me think I'm a slightly overdressed cowboy who never met a stranger. I do take my attire up a notch because that's part of how I get into character, but few who have met me in a professional environment realize that I am probably the shyest person in the room. Once you know it you can see it, as I can't stay in character the entire time at a conference. You'll see me over at the side, just quietly observing people. (If you do and want to come visit, that's fine with me. I'm not saying to leave me alone; I'm just doing what comes naturally.) One thing about doing this for as long as I have is the speed at which I can get back into character. Most people never see it happen, but I still have to make the transition.

I'm very shy, but I'm in our local little theater group. When I'm "on" and in character, I can do things I can't normally do.

That person has their finger right on it. I know you've heard people talk about when they are on, they can do this and that. It was a surprise for me when I started doing these programs and first found out there were people in my course who said "I am painfully shy," then later admitted they were very active in little theater or some form of entertainment. It turned out there was no limit to what they could do as somebody else, or, in other words, "in character." That is precisely the strategy we're going to pursue first.

DEVELOPING A PUBLIC PERSONA

 The idea of being "in character" intrigues me, and I can relate to the phenomenon from my days of vocal performance. Maybe you could assure me of something. When we are in our brave, bold character, do we sacrifice any of the intuitive or sensitive nature of our introvert? Are we in essence the same person, with the same sensibilities, or do we become an alter-ego like Professor Clump's skinny nemesis à la Eddie Murphy? (Apologies to those who haven't seen The Nutty Professor.*) I don't want to become an obnoxious toad in exchange for a bit more confidence. How will I know I am not being that alter-ego?*

Very good question. I suppose this could be a danger, but the neat thing about inventing a persona is that we can pick, choose, and design what we want.

When I fell into the hands of that speech teacher in college, and he convinced me that I could invent a public façade to hide behind, I had to give some thought to what that would be. It was simple. The created persona would be a compilation of character attributes of people I admired, maybe famous, maybe just friends. A major influence was a boy I went to school with. He was captain of the football team, president of the student council. Everyone admired him, yet he had just as much time for the quiet and shy as he had for the very popular. He wore his very strong faith not like a cross on his forehead but subtly, and made no compromises about it. I never heard him teased or ridiculed even by people who were known to do such things. I wanted my public persona to have that kind of presence.

Then I realized the boy I admired hadn't acquired his standing by taking from all of the positions and honors he held. Instead he used those positions to be a stronger servant to one and all.

Talk about following the example of Jesus.

I have had to reinvent my persona over the years. The character that I used when I was a successful Chamber of Commerce manager needed revision for that of a writer and that of a literary agent. And of course I have the standard daily operating personas as well.

> *I feel more introverted than not when you peel back the layers to see what's really inside. Put me with my writing buddies, junior high Sunday school kids, or my fellow Beth Moore groupies, and I'm fine. I even enjoy speaking to women's groups and have been told I have a gift for that. But send me to a networking gig for work, and I have to force myself to walk in the door and actually be social.*

I said up front that a lot of people have no need to actually invent some sort of character, but for some they need a stimulus to help them get into the character that can help them do what they want to do. Some go to extreme lengths to create this persona; others simply need a little something to help them shift gears. Among people who have needed more of a stimulus are those who actually dressed like characters in their books. There were a number who bought clothes which they felt really made them look the way a writer should look and wore them only when they were trying to get into the proper persona.

For those who have been in plays in school or little theater or the like, you know how much freedom there can be in getting out there and being someone other than yourself. That's exactly what we are talking about. We're talking about playing a part, the part of a successful writer. Do it right, and it projects a confidence that editors and agents will respond to. It will project a confidence that groups we speak to will respond to. If you have ever seen me in any of my workshops, do I appear nervous? I've had people come up and say they wish they could be that confident in front of a group not knowing that it scares me to death. But it doesn't scare my friend (my public persona), and he does it easily.

Can we end up with an alter-ego, a secondary self or personality, instead of the public persona we want as was mentioned earlier? Sure, if we don't design our character right. But that doesn't mean our public persona won't seem a little over the top to us even at that. It actually should, if we are shy enough. Our "friend" should be able to do the things we aren't able to do.

A lot of shy people do role-playing before they try a live-fire event. All we're talking is extending that role-playing into the event itself. Whether it is a little or a lot, whether we have to keep it up or after a small transition period we can do it without the need of a public persona, it can be a very valuable tool to helping us do what we need to do. Johnny Carson never outgrew his need to project his public persona and remained a very private person, as have I.

People will quickly discover whether creating a public persona is a tool they need, and if they do, whether they need a little or a lot of it. The more difficult thing is really believing they can do it, which is the entire crux of this matter. There is nothing I can offer that can cause that belief to happen. It has to come from inside.

This brings to mind a graphic I have on the wall in my office. It's a picture of a tabby cat sitting in front of a mirror. Reflected in the mirror is a full grown lion. Another version of the same thing shows a young man sitting on a pony and looking at the reflection in a pond, but instead of seeing his own reflection he sees the image of a tall, broad-shouldered Texas Ranger. In a panel beside it is a weather-beaten old cowboy on an equally ancient-looking horse. He too is looking at his reflection in the pond, but he sees . . . the young boy.

In the movie *Facing the Giants*, the father of the young kicker tells his son that his actions will tend to follow his thoughts. If he believes he can't do something, the chances are he won't be able to. If we genuinely do believe we can do something, the chances are much greater that we can. Of course in the movie, the young kicker sought and received God's help in his task.

There's a line from an old self-help book by Napoleon Hill that says, "Whatever the mind of man can conceive and believe, it can accomplish." I don't entirely subscribe to that; I lay more credit to faith and God's help. But there is a lot of truth to it anyway. Genuinely believing we can do something takes us a long way toward achieving it. But the reverse works as well. If we genuinely believe we will fail at something, we can get all the help in the world and will still manage to prove ourselves right. I'm looking for believers–converts. I'm looking for people who will say, "Yes, I can learn to play a role and to use that role to convince people that I am more confident than I feel."

Are we being false to others when we do this? I don't believe we are. We all have both sides to our nature, and this is simply a tool to help the more outgoing side that we have repressed for so long to be expressed.

GETTING INTO CHARACTER

&⁓ *So how do you get into this "other persona" to do the interview?*

For me to effectively switch personas I had to learn to dress different, wearing clothes I wore at no other time. I had to carefully envision this new person working a crowd, speaking to a group, standing up to do a Q & A session where I had no idea what might be asked but would have to respond to it. I tried it out first on some small sympathetic groups and family. I started to feel like I was really allowing him to take over, and I would admire how he did. He can be pretty good, but as soon as he isn't there, I'm shy Terry again. The good news is when you do it and it works, it gets easier and easier to make the transition. I can do it in a heartbeat now. At the next conference, see if you can spot shy Terry. He'll be there.

But the biggest thing most of us fail to realize is everybody wants to help.

Do you ever watch skating? Saundra loves it, so I see a lot of it. When somebody falls in the competition, what happens? The audience becomes so incredibly supportive it is amazing — applauding and encouraging the skater. People want people to succeed. It's the same when speaking to a group. People often just listen to a good speaker but become proactive when they realize someone is having trouble. They'll help if we allow it and if they realize we need it.

An old speaker's trick is to talk not to the whole group, but to a few who are giving positive feedback by their expressions. As I move from point to point, I change my focus until I find somebody else showing agreement. By the end of my presentation I will have "spoken to" several individuals throughout the room.

It works. I have many success stories from past workshops that prove it does. But there is one catch to it. It will only work if we can really, wholeheartedly, believe that it will and that we can do it.

    I wonder if part of the problem we are having understanding the "persona" or creating a character to "be" when we are pitching or promoting our writing stems from those nagging doubts that we really are writers.

Whew, that's gnawing on the meat close to the bone, isn't it?

Good comment, and that is probably part of it. What does it take to be a writer? It's simple: we write; that's it. People who are serious about their writing, people who are investing time in their craft and working at it, are writers and should not be ashamed to admit it publicly.

Now, being a published writer — that's the next step. I strongly encourage everyone to do short work and not just put all their efforts into getting a book out. It can take a long time to get traditionally published in book length. I did a survey a few years ago and asked some five hundred multi-published writers (more than one book traditionally published) how long it took to get their first book into print. Some were able to do it pretty quickly and some an abnormally long time, but the average was six years. My first was six years almost to the month.

That doesn't mean I was unpublished. I had a number of articles and short stories in print. I had done a weekly column in several newspapers. I had short stories in several anthologies and collections. I had a taste of success to keep my spirits up while I tried to get some book-length work out, and I was making money.

I also followed some early advice, advice that I also give writers. I queried both agents and editors. (Eighty-five percent of the people in the survey published before they got an agent.) I limited my publishing queries to smaller houses and left alone the larger ones that prefer to receive submissions from agents for when I got an agent.

It is easier to approach someone as a writer if we really believe we are a writer. But if we are serious about our writing then we need the affirming step of saying to people that we are a writer. And like I say, that's much easier to do if we are selling some short work.

In the beginning of my career I also wrote for non-paying publications to build my credentials. By writing short work, we can qualify ourselves if it helps by saying, "I'm a published writer, but I'm still working on my first book-length project."

OKAY, QUICK REVIEW.

BY THIS POINT WE HAVE:

bought into the idea of inventing a persona and are working on just what our writing persona should be,

realized we do need to actually plan how we want to project ourselves in some areas of our life,

discovered we don't find projecting ourselves to be a problem, but have some other areas we are waiting to get to, or

decided that I'm nuts and stopped reading.

CHAPTER TWO

MAKING
THE PITCH

When is a book ready to pitch?

When it's finished. When it is as good as you can make it. That doesn't necessarily mean we quit working on it. Someone asked me how we know when a book is finished, and I said, "When someone gives us money for it and makes us leave it alone." As we learn more and grow in our craft, we tend to continually fine-tune our manuscripts instead of taking the leap and submitting them. The reverse of this, of course, is to submit a book that is actually in rough draft form.

We hear that new authors must have their fiction manuscripts finished before they can submit. That's true. We also hear that nonfiction can be sold on proposal and a few chapters. Not so true. A very high percentage of people who start books do not finish them, or even after a good beginning do not end up with that good of a book. Editors know this. I recommend a first book be complete, whether fiction or nonfiction. Even a successful author changing genres is to a large extent starting over in the process. Editors want to see the entire book then, too.

I just completed a survey of editors, and in today's marketplace an astounding number of them want to see the book or know it is completed, unless the author is someone they have worked with before or is an author with a substantial sales record.

The following was a checklist for judges in a writing contest several years ago, and author Deborah Raney found it so helpful that she adapted it for self-editing her own novels. She gave me permission to reprint it here.

Submission Readiness Checklist

Opening – Is there a hook to capture the reader's interest? Does the book start in the right place, or is there too much backstory?

Characters – Are the hero and heroine vivid, likeable characters? Do characters have that "something special" which makes them come alive? Are they described well? Do they change and grow from beginning to end?

Pacing – Does the pacing flow throughout the book? Does the reader want to keep turning pages?

Dialogue – Does the dialogue sound natural and realistic? Does the dialogue build characterization and move the story forward?

Secondary Characters – Are the secondary characters believable? Do they provide a valid addition to the story?

Setting – Is a time and place established? Is the setting easy to picture without taking over the story?

Point of View – Is the POV for each scene wisely chosen? Are the POV transitions smooth and important? Does the writer avoid head hopping?

Style – Is the author's style unique and appealing? Does she have a voice all her own?

Clichés – Does the writer avoid clichés in plot, characterization, dialogue and narrative? (This doesn't mean tried and true plot devices can't be used. But they need to be done in a fresh way that makes you want to read on.)

Would you recommend this book to a friend?

Now let's talk about making the pitch itself and set the stage a little.

Some people go into pitch sessions as if they were afraid they would be killed and eaten on the spot. That's absurd. Cannibalism is against the law.

Actually, most editors and agents are nice people and really want you to do well. Even if they know immediately that what you are offering is not for them, most will try to make it a pleasant learning experience.

Agents and editors will generally recognize when a writer is making their first pitch and will probably take over and guide them through it. I had one appointment where a young lady was so nervous that when she sat down, she broke into uncontrolled sobbing. She was my last appointment so I asked her to go for a walk with me. This was at the Glorieta Conference. We walked down by the lake and talked about her family and my family and what she wanted to do with her writing. She didn't even know when I got her pitch out of her. Her manuscript wasn't really a fit for me but I managed to show her what she needed to do in other sessions, and I believe her other appointments went pretty well.

There are pitch sessions that will not go that well. We know difficult people are out there. Hopefully we will have some good sessions first. The odds are that we will, because there aren't all that many of these difficult people. But should a session not go well, remember that this isn't our problem. They are the ones who have the problem, so don't internalize it.

On the rare occasion that I was involved in a difficult interview as a writer, I said something like, "I'm sorry, I can see this is not a good fit for you. I'm sorry to have bothered you with it." Then I got up.

Such an abrupt ending to an appointment will often cause the person to see they have been rude, and they should change tactics immediately. If not, then we know this is a person we could not have worked well with anyway. We just need to make sure we don't make their problem our problem.

One person I recently talked to had this sort of bad experience, then spent most of the conference trying to change the problem editor's mind. While the need to do this is perfectly understandable, I did suggest that the time he spent on that editor would have been better spent making other networking connections and making other pitches. I believe he did have some success getting that editor to see things his way—or the editor gave lip service to it to end the dialogue. I'm afraid (knowing editors as I do) that it was the latter.

   I won't have my book completed by September but was advised to set up appointments and practice pitching. Do I tell them from the start that I'm just practicing?

It's fine to use a pitch session as a learning experience. I like to know up front, myself. I can help an author get more out of it if I do.

The biggest mistake newbies make is to take too much time telling about their project. If we use up all the time so the editor or agent has no time for questions, we missed a real bonding opportunity. They'll probably take a proposal from us after the conference and maybe the proposal will do better, but we wasted our pitch time. We need a one-liner — an "elevator pitch" — that grabs their attention, and we should have it polished and memorized so we can draw it like a gun without thinking about it. This can also be known as the hook or log line (twenty-five words or less. This same expanded version of the elevator pitch also goes in the query letter).

However, for an opening pitch during an interview or pitch session, we can have three or four short sentences. The purpose is still the same, and it isn't to summarize our story. *Our purpose is to catch their attention and get them interested in what we are there to talk about.* We should deliver our pitch, then shut up! Sit there, giving them our most businesslike smile, and by our silence and the expectant look on our cherubic faces convey to them that we have served the ball into their court and it is their turn. With this type opening, the remainder of the interview will hopefully be give-and-take and will probably result in the interviewer questioning us about our book. This is exactly what we want to achieve.

When we do this we have engaged them in the process. You see, when someone is going to be listening to pitch after pitch (I've heard as many as a hundred at a conference), it becomes really easy to tune one out if it isn't really speaking to you, and you already know you are going to be giving a courtesy response. The only way to insure that the interviewer doesn't tune out is to involve them and do not do all the talking.

I'm impressed by someone who makes me work. I'm bored stiff by someone who talks for fifteen minutes of a fifteen-minute appointment after I've quit listening at the five-minute mark.

Someone said that you should control the interview, and they were right. However, that doesn't mean we should question the interviewer — that can actually get a bit annoying. Instead, make them get their head in the game; force them to question us about the project, about our writing credentials, about our platform, etc. These are the things that should be in our proposal in more detail anyway, so we just want enough on each to interest them.

A speaker came to our local workshop group a few years back and taught a course on writing flash fiction. It intrigued me. A class assignment was to write one, fifty words or less in a complete story: beginning, middle and end. I found myself trying to decide if the word "the" was needed to reach my goal. She bought my story then and there, and published it in the Roswell Literary Review. I got a whopping twenty-five dollars for it. After that, I occasionally tried a piece in places that published flash fiction and had a few published. Allowed word count varies, but flash fiction is always very brief and terrific practice for learning to trim a log line or pitch down to the essentials.

A good pitch is so sharp and concise that it sticks in the interviewer's mind; it immediately alerts the person that it's something they've been looking for. That doesn't guarantee success of course, but it makes a difference in the agent or editor's attention and participation in the interview. It helps if we've done our homework; it also tells us whether this particular editor or agent has recently dealt with similar projects, which suggests they may be the right person for us. That would indicate a well-scheduled appointment.

Example: if we sit down and start pitching our science fiction, and the first words out of the agent's mouth are, "I wish you had noticed on my submission guidelines that I don't handle science fiction" (or some other genre), then our preparation has failed us.

I was the conference host for New York agent Donald Maass some eight or ten years ago. We spent most of the conference together. The evening before my actual appointment with him (I did not pitch to him while hosting him), I mentioned I was to meet with him the next day, and would have my other hat on. He asked, "Am I the right agent for you?" I told him that's what I was coming to find out. He said, "You should already know before we meet."

I spent that night on the computer finding out what I should have already known. At the time I was writing adult westerns, and he didn't handle them. I was about to waste his time. I told him at breakfast that he didn't handle what I wrote, and he said he knew that but it was important for me to find it out for myself. He said to keep my appointment, and we would talk about how to find the right agents and editors.

Be aware that there is such a thing as a courtesy response. The conferences are paying our expenses, and most of the time as a result we will allow an author to send us a proposal. If you did not interest me but I invite one anyway, that is a courtesy response. They have little chance of success. I have been known to tell someone that it isn't an area I work in so I wouldn't represent it, but if they wanted to send me a proposal, I'd be happy to tell them what I thought about the proposal itself. A lot of professional writers actually ask if the editor is really interested or if it is a courtesy response, and if it is the latter they thank them but say they'd rather save both of them the time.

People who are nervous about pitching are usually worried about the uncertainty of it, but when we force the interviewer to carry the ball as I said, we should be confident that we can answer all of the questions on our work. If we can't, we shouldn't let it faze us. There is always the old magic eraser: "Hmm, I didn't come prepared to answer that question, but I would love to find out and email you with it right after the conference." We'll be told to put it in the proposal when we send it.

There is another situation we need to be prepared for. Lots of times new editors are the ones to draw a conference assignment. Should we draw one, we could have to reverse the above situation and feed them the things we expected to be asked in quick sound bites. This can also happen occasionally if we draw an agent or editor who has had so many appointments that they are starting to become brain dead. If we are prepared for this contingency and help them out, they will appreciate it.

A SAMPLE INTERVIEW

So, can you show me how an interview might go?

Sure, something like this:
You sit down at my table and open with a good, compelling pitch. I'm thinking the genre could work, the plot doesn't sound overdone, and it seems to have a promise of some good conflict. I'm interested. **+ *points***

I ask what the word count is to see if it's in the ballpark of what editors are buying. **+ *points***

I ask what your writing credentials are (a polite way of asking if you are published). If some good credits **+ *points***; not a deal killer if you aren't published, but no points.

I ask if you have identified comparables (I don't like to say competition). The best way to show you have a market for your books is to say, "I have a following; my last three books have all sold over half a million copies each." If you say this and it is true, the interview is over, and I will offer you a contract for representation on the spot. If you can't say this, the next best thing is to have several books you can point to that you can genuinely say, "I write for the same readers that read these titles." That effectively identifies your target market.

Please note I did not say to claim, "I write like Mr. Famous Writer." Even if that is true, we don't want the editors spending their time thinking about whether it is true or not instead of evaluating you and your writing. We should never compare our writing itself to other writers. But it is quite acceptable to say that we write for the same reader base. Identify a strong reader base and convince me you have a good shot at selling them. **+ *big points***

Then I ask about your platform and marketing plan—do you have some identifiable groups you have access to, and do you have a personal marketing plan to sell to them? So let's say you do. I will then ask for a proposal, and through it I will find out more about the story and more about your writing. Most people do just the opposite and try to sell their book. An interview isn't the place to do that. Sell yourself. Try to bond with the editor or agent. + *big points*

You will note I haven't gone back to the story. An interview is too short to sell your story. The most to shoot for in regard to the writing is interesting the interviewer in the storyline and conveying that it might be appropriate for them. **You are there to sell yourself** and make the interviewer feel you are an attractive commodity.

> *Disclaimer: Not all editors and agents feel this way, and some may pursue a different line of questioning, so be prepared. If I get different answers to questions that arouse my curiosity, I may ask different questions.*

As I said, now I'll ask for a proposal, unless something has come out in the appointment that makes me think it's something we simply do not handle. You should recognize that the questions I ask you are a simple summary of what I want on the written proposal. The proposal is the sales document that sells the book to a publisher.

FYI, an agent simply can't write as good a proposal as their client. We can tweak it and put our brand on it, but the author is the one who should give an agent a base proposal to work from.

At this point in the interview, I will tell you how I work, what to expect in a response time, a little about the agency, whether I am considering your work for another agent in our agency other than myself. I will not decide on your book or writing until I've read that proposal. Even then, your best outcome won't be a contract, but for me to ask for the full manuscript. Why? Because some people write great beginnings but can't sustain it over a full manuscript. Some manuscripts die in the middle or have other serious flaws.

There, we just had an interview in a ten-minute format — a little more leisurely if it is a fifteen-minute.

What can you do to prepare for it?

Write a terrific proposal. Don't expect the editor or agent to take it with them since most of the time they won't. If an editor does ask for it and takes it, it is a very good sign as they are probably picking something to read on the plane. I don't take hard copy stuff at all, conference or otherwise, but prefer to work strictly on the computer. I try to run a paperless office.

Another disclaimer: Always check the submission guidelines.

Our agency asks for what we believe we need to have to make the proper pitch. Other editors and agents may ask for something different. Even within our agency two of us take online submissions only, while others request it differently. *Send people what they want the way they have asked to receive it.* Big time negative points if you don't because it indicates you didn't bother to read, or even worse, ignored the requirements. This is the uttermost professional courtesy, simply responding to the requested format.

If you ask if I want to see a sample, I may say yes as well. If I do, the interview is over and it becomes a reading session. Now instead of you establishing a personal relationship with me, you've taken yourself out of the equation, and it's all about the writing. Remember that most interviews will result in the opportunity to send a proposal. A good proposal will sell our writing but it will not make the personal connection we need to forge; instead, it allows the agent or editor to spend the time reading.

Editors and agents are different, and you have to go with the flow. But for me, this one-on-one time is a chance to bond with an agent or editor. Speaking as an agent, we are far more likely to want to work with people we like.

But when editors and agents are at a conference and getting

tired, a chance to read instead of working the interview can be very tempting. Even though they seem to be very interested in our writing and we want them to read it, in my opinion we are better served by interfacing with them and trying to sell ourselves, then selling our work when we send the proposal.

I can't tell you how important a strong proposal is. I want to be able to say, "Yeah, I could use that to sell this book." And some editors even want the full manuscript attached to the proposal. Seldom do agents want this however, and the full should never be sent unless it is requested.

Remember this, ten to fifteen minutes is not enough time to sell a book. It isn't going to happen. We want to get enough in front of the agent or editor to ensure a level of interest so they will invite a proposal. Proposals, not interviews, sell books. Our main job in an interview is to sell ourselves, to build a rapport.

The book is just part of it. Editors and agents are looking for clients who they think have the right stuff, who are going to be a saleable commodity. They want to feel an assurance the writer is going to be able to pitch and promote, and that they have a good platform. We need to give the interviewer a glimpse of that before we send the proposal, while they are likely to remember us, so they will be eagerly awaiting it. But never trust an interviewer to remember anything. They will probably be seeing more than a hundred submissions a month, so remind them where you met and mention anything significant that was said. They will appreciate it.

MODULES

The key to being confident in all these areas is our comfort level. When we are doing something we are comfortable with and are feeling competent to answer questions, we are able to project that confidence into our interviews. It is only when that comfort level does not exist that we have problems.

Whether I'm teaching a class, fielding interviews, talking one-on-one with participants, or speaking to a large group, my ace in the hole is a little thing I call "modules." If I were speaking to you in a situation, it would be as if I had big rack filled with index cards behind me, and printed on each card is a "module."

A module is a paragraph that I have refined over the years that speaks to a specific point or subject. I know them well because I use them a lot. When someone asks me a question, I think, "That's A-22," and I rattle it off sounding very prepared and intelligent. This is how I can stand in front of a group fielding questions with no idea whatsoever of what I might be asked.

Often they aren't an exact fit but I can take one that is close and adapt it. Then if I get a question I have no response for at all, I pull module Z-99, "I can't answer that right now, but if you'll give me your email address after class, I'll get back to you as soon as I get home." And I do. With Z-99 in my bag, I know I can handle anything.

If you haven't started building your collection of modules, I recommend it. The place I would start is with the individual paragraphs of your proposal. Insure that none of them are something we have thrown together just because it is called for. These little nuggets are absolutely vital. They are not only the building blocks for our proposal, but the information we call on to handle an interview professionally.

CHAPTER THREE

THE COVER LETTER

What happened?

Editors and agents will review well over a thousand submissions a year but are only going to have the ability to take a handful. It doesn't take a mathematician to see that most are going to be passed over as they look for that diamond amidst the gravel. And it isn't the quality of the story that is the deciding factor; it's really good writing that just happens to fit with the openings they have right at that present time. So a wonderful book that the editor just has no place for is not going to make it. Ever get the dreaded "not a good fit" note and wished the editor had told us what was wrong? They did tell us.

So if the point of a query letter or an interview is to get a proposal invited, then what is the point of the proposal? To answer all of the questions those people evaluating submissions use to toss out those which will not be contenders. I've seen editors at conferences working some submissions in spare time and have seen them open it, glance at the cover letter and put it back. Game over.

What happened? The opening of the cover letter probably indicated it was a genre they don't handle. It should have never been sent to them in the first place. These situations can be avoided by simply reading the submission guidelines for that particular person and following them. I've seen some of those same submissions just thrown away, which told me the people never got a response at all.

The principle for both the cover letter and the query letter (sent without a proposal) is the same. On many submissions this is the only part of the proposal that will be read and sometimes not all of it. What do I mean? The moment an agent or editor reads something that tells them the project is not right for them, they stop reading. One of the most common stopping points might be if you say in the first sentence what your genre is, and it is not a genre they handle. No point in going further.

First, of course, is the date. Be careful that the "automatic update" option is not checked if we use "insert date," or every time the file is opened it will put a new date on it instead of the date it was actually sent.

Next is the address block. We should never send anything to "the editor." That's the same thing as saying "occupant." We should know the actual name of the appropriate editor we're querying. And we should have done our research to see if our manuscript might be a good fit for them. Just reading through a writer's market guide, then sending queries to every publisher that lists our genre, is a waste of time and money. More importantly, it burns a number of bridges that with proper research might have produced good leads.

We should always have a subject line that contains the name of the book and your name to make it easy to identify.

The opening line is the most important thing on the page. It has one job: to make them read down into the letter. If we met the agent or editor at a conference and they invited the proposal, that invitation is the most important thing and should be in the opening. If there was anything vital about that appointment, this is where we remind them what it was.

The second paragraph (or the first one if we don't have some instance about which to remind the person) should be our elevator pitch or more likely the longer interview pitch. It should be just enough of our story line to interest the reader in looking at the sample chapters or synopsis.

The next paragraph contains writing credentials. Depending on what we have to offer in the way of credentials, the purpose of this is to show that we have done some writing, are very serious about it, and that we have completed projects.

Remember that getting published is a survival process, not a selection process.

Only by striving successfully all the way to the end can we achieve the results we want. Each point in the letter, each piece of the proposal, has only one job: to move the reader through the process. None of them can close the deal themselves, but any of them have the ability to convince the reader the project is not a good fit, thus ending its consideration.

Finally, we ask for the sale. In the case of a cover letter, that means we ask for the chance to discuss it with them, or the chance to send them the full manuscript. All of this effort, and what do we hope it will accomplish? We want them to turn the page and start looking at our proposal. All of the samples in this publication are from an old one of mine. It was successful, though I don't hold it out as an ideal example. I couldn't in good conscience use one from my clients.

SAMPLE COVER LETTER

Date

Name
Address
City, ST Zip Code

Subject: Agented submission of Beyond the Smoke, by Terry Burns

Thank you for requesting to see this proposal. I enjoyed meeting with you at XXXXXX Conference. Our discussion did indicate that this 50,000-word project might very well be a fit for your current young adult publishing program.

There were no teenagers prior to WWII. Before that time, kids went from what schooling they were going to get to working on the family farm or ranch, or, in the city, working in stores and factories. Kids don't realize that the things they read about in the old west, that many of those working the ranches, riding with the cavalry or on trail drives today would be considered teenagers as were most of the riders who were so glamorized with the pony express. Girls were very often married by the time they were fifteen. The worst killer in the old west, Billy the Kid, today would be a delinquent teenager. This is the story of two young people having to grow up fast with all the odds stacked against them.

My agent is Joyce Hart. As an agent in her agency, I have a substantial speaking platform of several significant audiences a month. I have a strong online presence by interfacing with all the major Christian writing groups, with a website that has over three million hits, and I am an aggressive marketer and promoter. I would love to send you the full manuscript or discuss the possibility with you.

Blessings,

Terry Burns, agent

Chapter Four

An Introduction To The Proposal

A good proposal will say more about our professionalism as a writer than anything else we do.

As I said earlier, being able to answer any questions that are likely to come up in an interview or pitch session is as simple as having a good proposal prepared and knowing all of the points contained in it very well.

So let's take a closer look at the all-important proposal. What is it? What's included in it?

The proposal is the sales document for the book and it includes the synopsis, among other things. Fiction and nonfiction require different proposals. (A complete list of the things that go into a proposal is spelled out in great detail at our website, *www.hartlineliterary.com*). A proposal contains all of these things plus the first three chapters of the manuscript with the formatting intact (all of the rest of the proposal is single spaced).

A good proposal will say more about our professionalism as a writer than anything else we do.

In sales it's usually good to have a gimmick or something that makes us stand out from the crowd, but this is not true in submitting manuscripts and proposals. Our goal is to make our proposal and manuscript look exactly like those being submitted by seasoned professionals. Should we happen to be unpublished, we want them to discover that fact late in the document and be happily surprised, not know it the moment they open the proposal. We want the writing to stand out.

Many writers simply do not take the time to learn to write a professional proposal, and they pay for it when they submit. They just throw something together, and it shows.

If the pitch opening the session is successful, and the editor or agent is thinking "this might be a fit," it's an open door for the writer to take advantage of or an opportunity to lose out, depending on how the writer handles it.

Just remember, the only job of the blurb is to open meaningful dialogue, and the time involved in an interview is too short to sell the book. Our main job is to sell ourselves and establish rapport. As an agent, if I leave a conference with several writers in mind that impressed me with having the right stuff, you can bet I'm really going to be looking for those proposals.

You see, the point of the proposal is to survive all the tests and challenges and become one of the half dozen or dozen proposals that are still on the desk after the pile has been worked. The manuscripts are now in play, and now — and only now — does the writing become significant. Historically, something like eighty percent of the submissions or better are gone, many of which not a single word of the writing was read because something else told that editor it wasn't a fit before they got to that point. That ought to make the importance of the proposal pretty clear.

➷ But shouldn't the agent write the proposal?

No. If a writer doesn't have a good proposal, he or she is probably not going to get an agent. Most agents will say they can't write as good a proposal as the author can. The author knows the work so much better. Now me, I can take a good author proposal and make it better, but it is terribly difficult for me to start from scratch and make one from nothing. It would take a really outstanding situation for me to feel motivated to want to try to do it.

➷ So what goes in a good proposal?

Let's dissect it a piece at a time. I'm going to use one of my own that I used to successfully pitch *Beyond the Smoke*, originally titled *I'll Settle for Sundown*.

Again the disclaimer: always send a proposal that complies with the submission guidelines posted by the agent or editor to whom you are pitching. They often differ; however, our agency guidelines are pretty standard, even more stringent than some, and should do for most purposes. I should point out that this proposal is now outdated and much of the information that is in it is different in new proposals.

As an agent, when I send a "Request for Proposal" in response to a query it looks like this:

> *Thanks for thinking of us with this project, it sounds interesting. We'd be happy to entertain a proposal on it per the submission guidelines at our website at www.hartlineliterary. com which shows exactly what our agency needs to receive in order to properly evaluate the work in terms of the markets in which we are currently working.*
>
> *A professional proposal is a single Word or .rtf document that is a quality presentation, yet preserves the proper formatting in the requested first three chapters to show how the actual work is formatted. We want to see if it's something we could easily base a submission on to sell an editor on the project. The three chapters give us a feel for the writing. The rest of the proposal gives us a feel for the marketability of the project, the platform and promotion ability of the author. We accept this file as an attachment to an email and do not accept hard copy submissions.*
>
> *We look forward to seeing more on this project and having the opportunity to evaluate it up against the markets in which we are currently seeking work. We are looking to fill the needs we know exist, as well as new market needs which surface daily.*
>
> *Terry Burns, agent*
> *Hartline Literary Agency*

What I expect to get is a single document, attractive and professional, that will sell me on the project and that shows the potential to be used to sell the project to an editor.

Problems can sometimes arise when the requested materials are sent in a bunch of separate files instead of in a proper proposal.Most agents and editors don't have the time and patience to go rummaging through a bunch of files hunting the things they need to evaluate the project.

At our website, we ask for the following:

Guidelines for Your Fiction Proposal
Your fiction proposal should include the following items (which can also be found on our website under Guidelines for Your Fiction Proposal):

Cover Letter
One-page "sell sheet"
Biographical sketch
Story synopsis
Market analysis
Competitive analysis
Marketing strategies (also known as platform)
History of the manuscript (if any; this is for the agent only)
The first three chapters (or the full manuscript if requested)

NOTE – a non-fiction proposal asks for a different set of items.

ᴄᴀ *Some agents/editors request a query, synopsis, and first three chapters or fifty pages for the proposal. If that's all they request in their guidelines, is that what we should follow or would it be more professional to go for the gusto and send everything you mentioned here?*

Follow the guidelines whether it is for less or more. For one thing, it shows you are paying attention to what they want and that it is being submitted specifically to them. Maybe even say, "I have a

proposal prepared, but per your guidelines I am sending . . ."
They might say, "Let me see the full proposal." If they don't, you
have shown you follow instructions.

> *I have trouble getting my sell sheet to hold the formatting
> when I send an email unless I send as an attachment.
> Since so many agents and editors refuse attachments for
> fear of viruses, how do you get a sell sheet with graphics
> to go as email?*

I suppose it's possible to save them in some sort of way so they
can be pasted into an email, but I've never seen anybody do it. If you
aren't tech savvy enough to do that, and I'm not, just put together a
simple text-only version and paste that in.

When I get a proposal pasted into an email, I write back and
say that I can't tell anything about their formatting, the proposal
is hard to read, and could they send it to me as a nice professional
attachment. Most of the scare over viruses in emails is gone, and I
don't see very many who are worried about that any more. The ones
who are simply don't want it by email at all but want a hard copy.
Tamela (coworker, Tamela Hancock Murray) and I don't do hard
copy. We want them sent as an attachment.

> *I've never had an ABA focused agent or editor request a
> proposal, only the synopsis and first three chapters or just
> fifty pages. Should I include a proposal packet with those
> queries?*

No, as I said earlier, send them exactly what they ask for in
exactly the manner they ask to receive it. I can tell you the single
worst thing to say to me is: "I have read your submission guidelines
but . . ." Whatever they say following that but is likely to make me
very unhappy.

CHAPTER FIVE

THE PROPOSAL, ITEM BY ITEM

What's next on the list?

W e've discussed the cover letter, so let's look at what's next on the list. (A copy of the complete proposal for Beyond the Smoke is found in the Addenda).

COVER PAGE

Include the title, author's name, physical address, email address, the genre of the novel (e.g. cozy romantic mystery, Civil War historical, women's fiction), and the length (word count).

ONE-PAGE SELL SHEET

A one page overview that summarizes our novel.

I personally don't care about the cover page, and if it is there, I generally move it back to be the first page of the sample chapters if I am reformatting the proposal to go out. But the sell sheet is terribly important. It is a page with the key information on it that an editor can pull out and take to a committee meeting to pitch the book. My sell sheet has an attention-getting phrase or question as a title in large type and a short summary (longer than the interview pitch but shorter than the two to three-page synopsis). This time the summary must capture the full major points of the story. Do not hold back the ending as a teaser.

My sell sheet also includes my picture and writing credentials (much shorter than the writing bio that will appear later). These are in a column down the side of the page. Remember that we're listing writing credentials for the author. We're not trying to tell our life story, aren't applying for a job — and ladies, too much about home and family here makes you look like a mom who has written a book instead of someone serious about writing.

Series Potential

Mentioning series potential opens the opportunity to make any deal a multiple book deal.

As shown in the example on the next page, these do not have to be written but can simply be a "concept paragraph" that shows they have been plotted or outlined, and perhaps have some sample chapters written. This would allow a proposal on the additional project or projects to be quickly submitted if they were to be requested. I don't like for too much time to pass between an editor expressing interest in something and sending whatever is necessary to satisfy that interest. Editors receive far too much material and it is far too easy to move a project from the front burner to the back . . . or even completely off the stove.

Biographical Sketch

List your writing experience, education, achievements, and prior publishing history.

When we go for that first job, the first thing the potential employer will ask for is our resumé or for us to fill out a job application. The purpose of both is to show our experience. Kids complain that everybody wants experience, but wonder how to get experience if nobody wants to hire them. Experience always has value. This never changes in business, and publishing is business.

If we don't have writing credits, we don't have them. So we go with education, achievements, whatever is closest, and make it brief. Don't dwell on it. But the bigger goal should be to get some credits as soon as possible.

What do the kids do? They get anything they can to be able to put something on that application form as soon as possible. We have to do that too, because no matter what our other credentials may be in the other areas of our lives, having no writing credentials puts us in the same position as these kids.

When I first started trying to publish, my bio was as simp.. as this:

> *Published as early as high school in a state-wide anthology, contributor to high school newspaper and the Pampa Daily News. Soon to receive BBA from West Texas State including English and creative writing courses, and have ten years of varied job history.*

That isn't much, but it was what I had. At the same time I was pitching manuscripts, I started trying equally hard to get publishing credits. I was working the market, looking for ways to get any credits I could to replace the measly ones I had. Many of my early credits were unpaid writing gigs for online magazines, and getting articles in newspapers and magazines. Searching for these jobs, trying to write and publish anything I could, made me into a freelance writer, and more and more I started getting paid. My first book credits were in anthologies and collections. But soon the credits were decent and led to my first book-length fiction contract.

But if you compare the lengthy write-up in my bio with my sell sheet, you'll see the sell sheet had only this much:

> *Terry has eleven novels in print including a three-book series from River Oak. He has work in thirteen collections, has four nonfiction titles for a total of twenty-seven books in print, and has published over three hundred articles and short stories. He has a strong platform doing over twenty major events a year as an agent and popular speaker. He has a strong online presence returning at the top of all major search engines with a website that has over three million hits with over 450,000 unique visitors. He's a member of the cooperative marketing group, the Christian Author's Network, and works with a dozen writing organizations.*

So the job is two-fold: to get a "starting" writer's bio, and to start building writing credits. The funny thing about building a writing bio is we start with what we can get. We build it and add to it, dropping weaker credits as we get better ones to replace them; then it starts getting smaller again as the credits get stronger. Finally, the ultimate introduction would be to say, "My name is Stephen King," or something equally as impressive.

I can just see King calling up an editor in the wee hours of the morning and saying, "I just had a nightmare, and I'm thinking about writing a book about a big dog that has rabies, and I'm thinking about calling it *Cujo*." Is that all the proposal he would need? I think so.

Some things are better listed as being part of our marketing plan rather than part of our writing bio. We will probably see that more clearly when we get to that part of the proposal. What we hope to make clear from our writing bio is, "I can write and publish," and we want our marketing strategies or marketing plan to say, "I know how to promote and I have a platform."

Build writing credits by writing short work.

It is important that our writer's bio says "business." A bio that tells about hubby and the kids and family info doesn't say writer. It says a homemaker has written a book. Certainly not a bad thing, but not what we are trying to convey.

I have a top ten list for reasons to do short work even if we are primarily interested in book length work:

10. To get positive feedback
Working strictly in the book market, particularly trying to get that first book published, can be discouraging.

9. To reduce wordiness
Writing shorter works is excellent for the development of any writer's technique.

8. To promote other work
Word of mouth is the best publicity and promotion, and a good way to get that word-of-mouth buzz is to get people to read something smaller. Most of the time when that occurs, a link can be inserted or a bio inserted that will point them toward longer work. They think if they like your style on the short stuff, they'll be willing to look at something longer.

7. To increase confidence
Trying to get started as a writer can be daunting, no doubt about it. Successfully writing shorter works can bolster confidence.

6. To increase name identification and visibility
We talked about creating that word-of-mouth buzz promoting other work, but getting some visibility can be very helpful before we have that other work to promote. Proposals always have a section on marketing capability and marketing plans. Showing a pattern of getting our name out through short work can prove we know how to promote.

ld contacts and connections: networking

rinding freelance jobs requires a lot of networking. As this network builds we find more and different types of contacts. Where do you find writing assignments or jobs? The Internet. I know, easy answer . . .but it's true! A quick search online for "buys on acceptance" or "buys on publication" or "writers wanted" are great places to start. You can find opportunity at:
http://writersweekly.com/,
http://fundsforwriters.com,
http://thedabblingmum.com/writing/index

There is a free newsletter dedicated to the sale of flash fiction and short-shorts. It's a good source of markets for these works, and anyone interested in subscribing can do so at the Yahoo group,
http://groups.yahoo.com/group/FlashFictionFlash/

There are a lot of good leads at this site.

Writer's Digest publishes a list of fifty fiction markets annually. Christian writers can find a list of such markets in Sally Stuart's Christian Writers Market Guide, or can find much of it at her site, http://www.stuartmarket.com.

Good short fiction markets are listed at:
http://www.ralan.com
http://www.writerswrite.com/paying

These are just samples of what an online search can produce on fiction markets. For me the best tool is Writer's Market. I have used the online version at www.writersmarket.com in addition to the printed version that is only produced once a year. The online version is searchable and contains web sites on most of the listings where more precise information can be found — information that can be accessed by clicking on the link found right in the guide. This is not free though; these features are available only to subscribers.

4. To win contests and awards to enhance saleability.

Instead of submitting to publications, we can submit to contests. Contests often include publication as part of the prize. When we are building a résumé of writing credentials, contest wins can look very good. There are an astounding number of contests that involve short fiction and award substantial prizes. While we have to be careful to avoid the scams that are surely in this area, there are a lot of quality contests offering some nice financial return. Many offer excellent feedback on submitted work and may be a good steppingstone to publication and name recognition. Then too, Winner of the XXXX Award doesn't look bad on the old writing résumé.

You can find some good lists of contests at:
http://tectonicdesigns.com/contest
http://www.writersdigest.com/competitions/The Writer's Digest Contest site.

Of course a search will turn up a variety of writing contests.

3. To learn our craft

We have to learn how to research markets, successfully query, and write proposals. It can take a long time to learn these skills querying book publishers and agents. We can expedite this process greatly by querying and doing proposals on short work while we work on that book. The process is the same, and it can teach us the skills we need to know to go after the big quarry.

2. Build our writing credentials

As I said earlier, when we come out of school and go after that first job, employers want to see a résumé of our experience — which we don't have — or we fill out a job application, which is nothing more than a form résumé for people who don't know how to type up a pretty one. Writing is no different.

1. Money — What does it pay?

Some of these markets pay very well, some pay a minimal fee, and very many of them do not pay at all. The tendency might be to immediately dismiss those that don't pay, but that could be a mistake. As I said, they can be very valuable in helping us build our résumé. That value is significant. Articles pay more than stories and are easier to sell because fewer writers want to do them. We can earn from a couple hundred dollars up to several thousand bucks doing articles, often on assignment. That doesn't mean money can't be made in short fiction too. Most of us spend a substantial period of time working on a book, some a year or better. How many articles and short stories can be written and sold in that period of time?

There are a number of sites that can be used to find markets for short work. Most of the time, I was hunting all over the place looking for article opportunities where I did not have a product; but as soon as I found the opportunity, I wrote something to fit and submitted it. I still do that quite a bit, only now I get contacts from people asking if I can write them X number of words on X topic. I can usually write and proof an article or short story like that in an hour or so. I subscribe to the flash fiction newsletter which is all about short work, and to http://freelancewritinggigs.com/webandprint/tag/writing-gigs/, which is all about paying gigs for freelance writers. A friend of mine is a *New York Times* bestselling romance writer, but she has a couple of manuscripts in other genres she has been unable to sell. What's the deal? The way publishers see it, fan bases are not necessarily transferable. Someone with a romance following may not translate their fan base over to a nonfiction book or a drastically different genre. It's the same with nonfiction writers trying to break into fiction. A bestseller in one genre is a newbie in a completely different line. However, writing credentials are writing credentials, and hers still say she can finish work and meet deadlines. She just has to convince an editor she can make the genre shift and attract a whole new reader base.

For those of you who are trying to break into full-length fiction, I highly recommend submitting some stories to the newspaper, a *Chicken Soup* book, or a magazine to hone your skills and to get some practice dealing with editors, submission guidelines, and (as much as I hate to say it) rejection.

MARKETING STRATEGIES

The submission guidelines next ask for Marketing Strategies. This includes both the marketing plan and the platform. A marketing plan spells out what we plan to do to help sell the book. There are certain things we hope the publisher will do, depending on the publisher and how much marketing support they give, but the marketing plan says that regardless what the publisher does, this is what *we* plan to do. The platform is the access we have to various groups or entities that can help us promote and grow our visibility and, of course, that will be an avenue for sales.

People often define platform as the subject on which the author speaks, and what they'll base their promotion and speaking efforts on. But I like to define platform as the stage we stand on to do our promotion. Who's out in front of our platform is important.

If it's family and friends, it's a small platform. If we're well known in the community, the platform becomes a local one. From there, the platform can be regional, state, national or international. Who is it we have access to? This specifies our platform. These terms tend to get intertwined:

> **Subject** – what we are going to talk about or our area of expertise
> **Market** – age group and genre of our target market
> **Platform** – groups or touchpoints to which we have access
> **Marketing Plan** – how we plan to contact the groups to which we have access

Platform isn't about subject, although the subject affects it; it is about people. One of my clients has a national platform as a parenting expert. She does workshops and blogs and writes books and articles, etc. Her subject of parenting is what gives her the platform, but it isn't the platform itself.

A platform is all of the groups we have access to.

Someone else may write romantic suspense, but they have a large platform because of an expertise in political affairs. That's the subject, but it isn't the platform. The platform is all of the different avenues of people they have access to because of the things they are doing in connection to the subject.

Agent Chip MacGregor had a good definition in his blog:

> *An author's platform is the collection of touchpoints the writer has with other people. Does he have a TV show? Is she on the radio? Does he have a busy speaking schedule? Is she a recognized expert in a particular area? Does he have a popular blog? Is she a regular columnist in a newspaper or on a popular website? You add up all those touchpoints,*

*and you've got the author's platform. In many ways,
the author's visibility, and it reflects the author's ability
to attract readers to a book. That's a platform. As to how
to build one... it's going to be unique for each author. I
suggest you ask yourself what you can be known for, and
how you can expand your points of contact with other
people. For some, that means establishing a speaking
schedule. For others, it means writing articles and getting
them posted on blogs and e-zines. For still others, it means
becoming the go-to guy when the media need an expert
on a particular topic. Your platform will be different
from everyone else's. (MacGregor, Chip. "Marketing and
Platforms." Posted April 24, 2009. www.chipmacgregor.
com.)*

So what kinds of things comprise a platform? If we're in a lot
of online writing groups, Facebook and Twitter; if we blog; if
we have a well visited website; if we write a newspaper column
or contribute to a significant magazine; if we have friends and
family, know people at work, or maybe throughout an industry.
You see where this is going? Each thing I mentioned has a group
of people connected to it, and each is a different group (with
some overlap, of course), but the sum total of all of the various
avenues that we have access to are the people standing out in
front of our platform.

Let's say our publisher is going to do some good distribution
for us, and they are going to have sales reps selling us into stores.
The next question becomes how do we get off that shelf and out
the front door? Chances are the amount of advertising will be
slim, and for us to just depend on impulse shoppers is not a good
idea. Most people buy books because of name identification.
They have bought the author before and liked them, so they'll
buy them again. But what if we are new on the market? That's
where platform comes in — avenues we have access to and

can start working to build a buzz, start growing some name identification.

When they talk about the market they are aiming for, a lot of people say their book is for both male and female readers from eighteen to eighty. They think that's a huge market, when actually that is no market at all. We all want to sell our books to everybody, that goes without saying. When we name a market, a publisher wants to know if there is a specific group or groups that we have some good access to, which brings us back to platform.

A lady at a conference a while back gave me the "everybody" response and just didn't believe it when I told her that wasn't a market at all. The book was nonfiction and, if I remember correctly, had to do with some sort of child abuse. I asked if there were organizations for that and if there were online groups and other such contact points, and she said yes. I told her that was her market. She could go ahead and try to sell everybody else as she got a chance.

Sometimes I hear "bookstores and on Amazon." Again, that's just where books are. Impulse purchases from just seeing your title on the shelf are a long shot. Most of the time, "sales" means somebody advertised or promoted or in some manner told people the book was available. That brings us back to identifying and working special markets. Publishers can tell if a group we identify is really a market, and they can tell if the means we're suggesting to contact them by is really a viable option.

    ❧ *I identify my target market, or audience, as women ages 18-35. I don't think that is too broad . . . is it?*

That depends. Do you have a strategy for contacting everyone in the country in that age group? Sure, we all hope they'll pick up our book, but we're talking about sales. Platform is identifying the people or groups that we have access to in order to sell books. "Women eighteen to thirty-five" is fine for a market-definition genre sort of thing, but in a marketing plan it is too generic unless we have the means to contact them all. Where are these women that this lady can access them? Church? Women's clubs? Online groups? Friends? Relatives? These are markets, and once we have identified such a group or groups, then we just have to ask ourselves what specific ways we have to contact them. Perhaps we're members of the group, maybe they have newsletters or magazines or meetings, maybe we have access to them that outsiders don't have.

My current book is a Young Adult. Do I say my platform is all young adults? No, I don't have the means to contact all of them. My platform identifies some groups I do have the means of contacting, and my marketing plan says how I plan to contact them. If I had a regular program aimed at teens on the Disney Channel, then could I say my market is all YA kids? No, but I would have a national platform identifying Disney Channel watchers as one of my groups.

    For most of us, we will need to work slowly, steadily, and purposefully to build a platform by joining groups, identifying markets and building contacts, contacting publications, and writing, writing, writing. It sounds daunting.

I don't see that as daunting. Everyone already has a platform unless they are complete hermits. The place to start is to identify the platform we already have. Everyone has friends and relatives, and how about the directory of our church? I'm guessing that's four hundred to five hundred names right there. Do we have work contacts? How many people are on the various groups we're in? ACFW is somewhere between fifteen hundred and two thousand by itself. Involved in a PTA group? Can we write a letter to the editor? See, I've named up in the thousands in a platform that is mostly local and very average.

But we're close to a few of these people, so we take them into our confidence and tell them we could really use their help. We get them to agree to send a postcard about our book to ten friends. A lot of them will do it, and it puts the bug on them to get the book themselves as well. Then we ask them if they'll also request their local library to acquire it. In how many different towns do we have friends and relatives? Libraries tend to acquire books that local people request because few ever request them. It isn't an accident that I'm shelved in close to two thousand libraries, and every one of those books is going to be read fifty to a hundred times, generating name recognition in a new town.

Visit blogs and leave comments, submit short work for money, even for free if necessary, to get your name out. These are just simple beginning steps, but they work, and most of them can be done very quickly. Sure, work on the bigger and stronger contacts first, but also get a number of the smaller projects going, and do it fast.

We can gather ideas on platform building from the vast amount of information available to us today. Keep your eyes open for opportunities to expand your visibility and "buzz" or name recognition. This will help you with your marketing.

Isn't it costing you potential sales to have a book that can be checked out from the library?

I doubt it. Most voracious library readers check out books because they read more books than they can afford to buy.

My book is aimed at women 13-35.

Here we go again. This does indeed identify the age group of our readers and is our target market, but it isn't our platform unless we know how to reach every one of them. Personally, I couldn't afford to buy that much advertising, and it is doubtful I could convince the publisher to do it. We need to break it down from that general market into target groups where we have access to a number of these women. A college sorority? Women's club? Library book discussion group? An ad in a magazine that specifically targets this age group might identify enough of them that they could be considered a market group.

A publisher will have means of targeting just the age group, but a personal marketing plan targets the portion of the age group that we actually have access to. The total of these identifiable groups is our platform, and the means we have of contacting them is our marketing plan.

> *I'm not getting it. I had one publisher respond to my query and ask me to send some info regarding my audience (that's where I came up with the women 18-35). However, I now understand that that was a wrong response. What I'm not understanding is, what is the right response?*

Let's try it this way. Eighteen to thirty-five is correct for the portion of the reading public that you feel would read the book. But by itself it tells a publisher little. That's a really big group of people. It isn't a wrong response, it just isn't enough response.

> *In addition to the age group that I mentioned, I also said I thought people who read Karen Kingsbury, Susan Meissner, and the contemporary works of Lori Wick would enjoy the novel. Is that right?*

These are comparables, and that narrows down that eighteen to thirty-five target group considerably. You are saying that these individuals identify the base of readers within that group which you are writing for and hope to sell to. A publisher should understand who this reader base is. More importantly they will know whether or not this is a group they service.

The people listed below are part of your platform. They are groups you have direct access to. Once again, this is narrowing down your eighteen to thirty-five target group into something manageable and marketable.

• Member of ACFW and ACW
• Alpha Xi Delta Alumnae
• Hillsdale College Alumnae
• Social Networking -(Facebook/LinkedIn)
• Contacts with area churches
• Contacts with local school districts
• Contacts with local newspapers, television and radio stations

Chances are, the means you will use to contact each group named in your platform is different, plus, to the extent of your ability, you will have contacts aimed at the general public trying to get what you can from casting the big net.

The marketing plan involves all of these various means. For example, you might choose to communicate with ACFW via email, in person at the convention, and by having a blog which you would encourage them to visit. For the sorority, you might decide to use letter-writing or possibly use a sorority newsletter or magazine, trying to create a buzz by getting friends within the sorority to contact others within the group on your behalf and so on, depending on how you think you have the ability to use these various groups to market the book. The bottom line of marketing is to make local, general public contact efforts.

Sticking to the initial example, you are saying you don't expect to sell to the entire world, but only to eighteen to thirty-five year old women. That doesn't help a publisher much because that is still such a large segment of the population; but you can further identify the reader base by using comparables. By using the three which were listed, a reader base is identified which the publisher can see and understand.

THE PROPOSAL, ITEM BY ITEM

Finally, in the marketing plan, you show that you can contact both individuals and groups you know, and how those plans differ for each group.

❧ Can you tell us what your platform is?

I do twenty to thirty major programs and workshops a year all across the country. I have a database of over eight thousand names of former book purchasers, friends, family, work related, church related, etc., all people whom I can direct mail. I was in Chamber of Commerce work for nearly thirty years, and I'm well known in those circles in the state and, to a degree, nationally. I have a very visible online presence in twenty-four different groups, and have a website that returns at the top in all my significant categories and has very high traffic. I've worked closely with and have cultivated library connections nationwide. These things and others combine to give me a national platform, although certainly not as large of a national platform as someone with name identification on that level. I have cultivated a list of over a hundred book reviewers and can approach them for reviews.

This marketing section demonstrates to the publisher that I have access to tangible numbers of people. I'm not promising that I can sell to them, mind you, but I have access to them. The marketing plan shows that I'll try to take advantage of this people-access to sell books. More importantly, it shows my attempt to build name recognition. I have a small but loyal fan base; those who read my books tend to like them and will read more if they get the chance.

What size marketing plan should be in the proposal? What I've included here only hits a few of the highlights. My actual marketing plan is very detailed and runs over twelve pages. It is stated in very specific terms because it's what I'll actually use in my marketing efforts. The publisher doesn't need to know that much detail, maybe a page or so. I may not even share my full marketing plan with them after the book is under contract, maybe with the publicist or PR people, or possibly just share individual items as I do them. I do know that the more I do and tell them I'm doing, the more likely they are to match or exceed my efforts. Mostly in the proposal they just need the broad strokes.

You mention book reviews, how do you go about getting them?

There are different kinds of book reviews and they can be vital. The best are the industry reviews such as *Publisher's Weekly, Booklist,* or *Midwest Book Review.* The publisher generally has to set up these reviews, and often they have to be done before the book is in print.

Why are these reviews so important? Buyers for bookstores, and particularly for chain stores, simply do not have the time to read all the books necessary for them to buy in order to stock the shelves. That means they depend upon two things: the cover, and how well they think it will display and attract readers; and industry reviews for sources they trust. They don't read the books; they read the reviews. Librarians also select books largely based on industry reviews.

The second kind of review is peer review, and there are tons of them available. We can find out about them from various online groups or by a simple search of book review blogs. They generally have to be provided a book in order to get the review. A whole series of these are known as a blog tour, and there are several places that are organized in a way to provide blog tours. Some do so for a fee and are aimed primarily at the publishers themselves. However, an author can spend some time finding and building a list of review sites and, in essence, putting together their own blog tour.

❧ I see you have a lot of library placements. How do you get these?

Some publishers publish almost exclusively for the library market and libraries do prefer hardbacks. Some in fact will not shelve paperbacks. However, there is a process that libraries can do which strengthens the paperback covers so they can stand the increased service, and a majority of libraries are prepared to do that.

The number one way to get into libraries is to be reviewed by *Booklist* and a couple of other places that libraries use to identify books (discussed above). However, the author can go after this market themselves if the publisher does not do so—and a surprising number of publishers don't bother. Some authors don't want to bother either, saying they don't like the idea of selling one book to a library for a bunch of people to read instead of selling all of them books. Actually, heavy users of libraries do so because they read more books than they can afford to buy, so I don't believe we do give up those sales; rather, we get our name out in a new community and start creating that buzz that is the most important marketing of all. In addition, most people buy books through name identification and, if we get them to read something of ours, they are more inclined to buy other books we've written.

So how can the author do it themselves? Go to http://www. publiclibraries.com/ and you will find all of the libraries in the country that have an online presence. We can actually click on to their card catalog in most and see if they have us shelved. If they don't have us shelved, some will allow a book to be suggested online. Even more can be sent a solicitation letter suggesting they acquire the book for their collection. The surest route, if we have a friend or relative in the community, is to ask them to request the book be added to the collection. A patron request is the strongest route to a library shelving.

I actually keep on my website a list of the places I have found my books shelved. It is by no means a complete list but does represent nearly 1900 libraries. Library books reach a minimum of fifty people, which means I have reached over 100,000 people through libraries in addition to my normal sales and distribution. To me it is well worth the time trying to increase library shelvings.

Market Research and Analysis

This is an area of the proposal in which many just slap something down, but if we do we miss a great chance to make a real difference in the decision process. An editor can read the writing for themselves, they know what your writing credentials mean, but this is an area they don't know about. If we don't say anything, it won't hurt us very much other than just making it look like we aren't following instructions. But if we really tell them something at this vital point in the decision process, it would make a major difference.

It's the big "will it fit" question that we hear over and over, and this is our chance to say something directly about that. If they don't think it's a fit then they probably aren't even going to read it. Why would we take a chance on making that cut without even taking a shot at helping them decide?

The key to publishing is both knowing and being able to demonstrate who our reader base is and making a strong case that we can market to them. The best way to do that is to say, "My last three books all sold over 200,000 copies." But if we can't say that, what then?

We tend to think about this process backwards. Sure, it's semantics, but understanding the difference can be important.

The bottom line for editors is their reader base and whether or not they will read the book, story, article, poem — no matter what the writing product may be. Editors know who their readers are and what they are reading. They may occasionally take a chance on stretching the envelope if they've had a lot of recent success and feel they can afford to try. Most of the time, however, they have to stay comfortably within what they know their readers want to see.

That means as writers we have to demonstrate that we know who our readers are. We have to define them and make a strong case that we can sell to them. As I said, the best way is a proven sales record, but if we don't have that, we have to prove and define our reader base another way.

We look for comparables, authors and publishing houses that are selling to the readers we feel are our market. We should never say we write like popular writers, because even if we compare favorably we don't want the editor spending time comparing the writing instead of evaluating the story. But it is good to point out what it is about their books that make us think they are comparable and then how our book differs from theirs.

We just have to be sure that we are talking about the reader base, not about the writing. We are talking about comparable authors and books, but only to use them to demonstrate and prove the reader base. It is all about the readers, and editors and agents understand that.

How do we prove we can sell to these readers if we don't have an established sales record? We can't prove it, but that's where our sales ability comes in. We have to convince that editor that we can do it. Other good publishing credits can help.

How do we find this reader base? Read, research, hunt for comparable writers. It doesn't have to be similar writing, maybe not even the same genre. The key is, can we honestly answer *yes* to the question, "If readers like this book, will they like mine?" No salesman can do a good job of selling a product they don't believe in, and we can't make a case for a book being a comparable if we don't really believe it is. If we can find honest reasons for our comparables, an editor may believe the same thing.

   ℳ I write medieval. There really are not any comparables in the Christian book market.

A comparable is authors and books you can point to and say with assurance, "Readers who like these books will like mine." If you can't find direct subject comparisons, find authors you feel are selling to your readers. Next to liking the writing, an editor wants to identify the readers and feel like they can sell to those readers. Your statement tells me there aren't any readers, so why should I be interested in the book? We must be able to confidently show them readers if we expect them to actually look at the project. So don't explain to me why there aren't comparables–never tell an editor there are no comparables. We think we are telling them a book is unique, but they read it as admitting there is no market. If we want them to seriously look at our manuscript, we have to show them there is a reader base for it.

   ℳ Most of the people writing Biblical fiction are big names. Francine Rivers and Jerry Jenkins, among others. I felt so nervous about comparing myself to them. Now I know I am just saying that people who like their Biblical fiction will be the ones who will buy mine. Right?

Exactly right. I could say I write like Jerry Jenkins, but that would sound ludicrous and would probably get me rejected just on the face of it. But saying I write for the same people who buy his books does not sound ludicrous at all, and I'm not claiming I will sell as many, just pointing out how many there are to sell to.

   ℳ Should our comparables only be works that are read by the same readers, or be things that are similar to our work but appeal to a different audience? Allow me an example: I recently found, through research for this section, a comic book geared toward 10 year old boys that uses a similar format to my YA (12-18) novel. Would that be something to use to say, "There is this out there and mine is similar on points A, B and C but different on D, E, and F"?

You are dissecting it and comparing the writing. The purpose of comparables is not to compare writing but to define the reader base. Since we can't prove our reader base with sales numbers, we define them by pointing out other books that are being written for the same readers. If the editors are familiar with these books, then they are familiar with who the readers are. But then you start comparing the writing, and now we're talking about books instead of about readers. We just need to be asking ourselves, "Are these the readers that I'm writing for? If they like this will they like mine?" We are looking to say, "I am writing for the same readers that are reading these books," then name several.

෴ *When I first started working on a proposal a year ago, I went to a Christian book store and told them I was doing market research and asked if they could help me. The gal told me to spend time in the section of my genre (romantic suspense), write down titles/authors, and come back to her when I was done. I spent quite a while pulling books off the shelf and ended up with a list of about a dozen I thought might have the same reader base as my WIP. I took the list to her and, bless her heart, she looked up every one of them and showed me their sales record (in that specific store) for the past year. The range of sales was from none (ulp!) to decent to nice. I didn't include any blockbusters, though now I see that I could have since I was going for reader base. Anyway, I bought several of the ones selling well so I could continue to familiarize myself with my genre, and took the list home. From there I went to Amazon.com, looked up the books on my list that were selling well (I assumed if they were selling well in this particular store, they would be across the nation), read the blurbs and reader comments, and selected four novels as my comparables. Whew! Quite an effort, but worth it.*

Very nice job and a good strategy for identifying comparables.

     Here's how marketing analysis works: when I saw that your stories would be enjoyed by those who like Stephen Bly (and others like him) I knew I must read your stuff. That worked! I love books by Stephen Bly. That is just plain fun reading.

I was once asked if the age of the book matters when it comes to being a comparable. I have all of Louis L'Amour's books and enjoy reading them. I'm sure that influences my writing, and I feel like those who read him will enjoy mine. Old books? Sure, the man has been dead like twenty years. Still work as a comparable? You tell me—he still continues to dominate the western book racks.

     It seems to be a lot of papers to send to an editor. Do they take the time to read this many things? And when one gets to meet with editors at conferences, if that editor is interested right there on the spot, will they want all this in a packet to take with them? This seems like so many pages. I want to be within reason. Can I ask how many pages you would have in your proposal packet?

It is a lot to send editors, and no, they won't read all of it. They will look up the portions of it that interest them and the more it interests them the more they will look up. However, since we don't know what they will look up and what they won't, we had best send them everything they ask for in their guidelines, right?

How big will it be? Given the fact that it contains the first three chapters or around thirty pages of writing, then it contains five to ten pages of proposal, an average proposal might run thirty-five to forty pages, which is about where mine will run. You will want to have a couple with you at a conference just in case, although it is unlikely they will want to carry it back. If you are lucky, they won't ask to look over it and spend your precious interview time reading.

   Why should the author do this [find comparables]? Why isn't the agent doing it?

Actually agents are working on it, but chances are the author is reading more, and particularly reading more in their field than the agent has time to do. I guarantee as a writer I know which authors I am most comparable to. Not write like, never write like, but I believe write for the same readers that they write for, therefore they help define my reader base. As an agent I try to understand this for my clients, but most of the time they have a better feel for it than I do. They get far more time to read books that might be comparables than I do, plus they are only looking for one set of comparables where I would have to be looking for over sixty sets.

WRITING THE SYNOPSIS

Most people give too little or too much information in a synopsis. This isn't a scene-by-scene analysis of the book, but rather the major story points showing how the story develops, the high points and of course, how it ends. Two to three pages is what most editors and agents want to see, some would rather it even be a single page. I have seen some ask for a chapter by chapter synopsis, but that is usually just for nonfiction and although I have seen it, it is rare in fiction submission guidelines.

Some editors and agents will read the synopsis before anything else. Some don't read them at all. Some will read the sample chapters, then if the writing appeals to them, they'll check out the synopsis.

A synopsis is always written in present tense. Clean and neat is the key, spare the details, just cover the plot points. An entire scene is at most a sentence or two, but don't just recite the bare bones; state each sentence to catch the reader and move them through. Begin with a hook and identify the main conflict and the theme. The object is to boil your story down to a quick summary that is a fast and interesting read. We don't want a synopsis that is just a dry recitation of facts.

I think it helps if you know why an editor or agent wants to look at a synopsis. It quite simply tells them if you appear to have carried the story through all the way to the end.

CHAPTER SIX

MAKING THE CUT FOR THE TWENTY PERCENT

*"Getting published is not a selection
process but a survival process."*

You remember I warned that getting published isn't a selection process. Let's recap: To do a good job pitching and promoting, we had to first be able to feel confident to make the presentation. The key to that was developing a writer's persona which allowed us to present the side of our personality we wanted editors and agents to see; a little fine tuning for some, all the way up to a major character development that we can learn to hide behind for very shy people. We discussed how to prepare for the pitch session or conference by developing a one-line elevator pitch, or log line, that we could draw like a gun. We mentioned a slightly larger version, the size of a small paragraph, for use in the query letter, to open an interview where we had a little more time than the one-liner, and to use on a sell sheet.

We dissected the sell sheet and the proposal. We put together a good two to three-page synopsis which may or may not be read, or may be read at any point in the process. We learned how to state what our market is, what our comparables are, and what we want those listings to say about our work. We learned that a ten or fifteen-minute interview is not enough time to sell a book. Our main task is to first get a proposal invited, then to sell the editor on us as writers. We want them to like the proposal when it comes in because of our professionalism and because we have convinced them that we have the ability to promote and help market the product. In short, we show an editor or agent that both we and our writing are saleable products. Hopefully our interview resulted in an invitation to send a proposal.

We have impressed the editor, and we have crafted a great proposal to send them. So now we have survived our way through the maze, and it's all about the writing, right?

Not quite.

Let's go back to our mantra for this course: "Getting published is not a selection process but a survival process."

Now our task is to survive all of the little tests and decision points that occur when our submission is opened (whether hard copy or email file, depending on submission guidelines) in order to end up one of those dozen or so left on the desk which will duke it out for that available catalog slot or two. We need to look at some of those tests and make sure our proposal and our manuscript can weather them and get into that final selection process.

So, let's talk about the manuscript itself, particularly those critical sample chapters that are part of the proposal. Hopefully, we have done our homework and research and have our proposal in the right hands, because if there is nothing else we get out of this discussion, we need to lock our minds around this: the biggest secret to publishing is the ability to get the right product to the right person at the right place and the right time.

There are bestseller-quality manuscripts that will never be published because the people who wrote them never made this elusive connection. On the other hand, we all know some books that were printed which leave us wondering how in the world they ever made it into print. The only reason for that is that it was the right subject, and it hit the right person at the right place and time. Maybe we send a much better book on the same topic soon after the other has been purchased and is on its way to press. Since ours is much better they'll stop the presses and publish ours instead, right?

No. Hitting all four of these — product, person, place and time — correctly is the whole game. Miss any one of the four, and it's no sale, no matter how good the manuscript is. It's like a jigsaw puzzle that has several dozen pieces, and if one is missing the puzzle can't be finished — which means publishing doesn't happen. Most of the time these pieces are not all there. We're hunting for that elusive place where all the pieces fit. That's what this entire discussion will be about.

Patience is a key. How long does it take? The average time in my survey was six years. Why should it take that long? As I said, most of the time the pieces don't fit, and it takes time to find the place where they do.

So, how do we improve the odds? How do we rule out sending to the wrong places? How do we give our manuscript a better shot when it gets there? We need to keep surviving those tests until the reading starts. And the first test when it comes out of the envelope or when that email file is opened is whether or not the manuscript is professionally formatted. I have a good checklist I use to make sure mine are ready to go, and I'll share it with you here.

IS IT READY TO SUBMIT?

One large hurdle to publication is submitting a professional-looking proposal or manuscript to an agent or editor. The object here is not to stand out, but to look like an established pro. A submission which appears as though the submitter does not know what he or she is doing, or which looks like it will take too much work to get ready may receive little or no attention. These rules cover the primary items for the formatting of the manuscript, but the submission guidelines posted by the editor or agent you are submitting to should be the guide. While it is true a manuscript might not be rejected for breaking only one of these rules (unless it's a glaring one), a combination is sure to catch attention. We have to prepare a manuscript in some manner anyway, so we might as well prepare it right.

CHECKLIST FOR FORMATTING A MANUSCRIPT

One-inch margins all around, double spaced in New Courier 12 or Times New Roman 12 font, on one side of the paper only. To insure a consistent number of lines per page the widow and orphans feature should be turned off. Paragraphs should be indented .5 inch with no blank line between paragraphs. They should never be indented by spacing in (these have to be removed by the editor). A tab is acceptable, although the preference is to go into paragraph formatting and just select first line indent.

One space between sentences. Do not justify the right margin.

If tracking changes have been used during the preparation process, these should be completely removed and not just "hidden."

Chapters should begin near the center of the page (sixteen blank lines), and a formatted page break should be inserted at the end so chapter headings stay put if changes are made. Chapters do not require titles. Using a section break (new page) instead of clicking on "insert page break" can cause problems in the formatting.

There should be a header with author's last name, a word or two from the title and the page number in the upper left or right of the page. This should be in the header and not in the text so it does not move when text is changed. Make sure under "layout" that "first page different" is checked so the header appears only on subsequent pages.

The cover page on the front should have the title in normal size type, centered halfway down the page and double spaced below it, your name or byline. Your name, address and contact information in the upper left or lower right. Contact information should include phone number and email address, but should not include social security number.

The word count (rounded off) should be in the upper right

hand corner. Word count for many years was determined by multiplying the industry standard 250 words per page times the number of pages. Most houses now use computer word count.

A forced scene break (intentional white space) should be indicated by centering the pound symbol on a line of its own.

Do not include drawings, colored type, fancy fonts, giant size type on the cover, or anything else to make your manuscript stand out. Remember the goal is to look professional, not different.

Italics may be indicated by underlining, although most now will just take them inserted as italics where they go.

Remember that regardless of what is being submitted, the first paragraph or two must capture the interest of the reader, editor, or agent by raising a question or arousing curiosity to cause them to commit to reading further down into the manuscript.

Replace passive verbs with active verbs (was, -ing verb forms).

When ready to submit, the proposal itself will be single spaced, but the sample chapters should be placed in the proposal retaining their formatting so the editor or agent can insure the manuscript formatting is ready to go.

Finally, individual places where you wish to submit may have requirements particular to how they wish to receive a submission. Always check submission guidelines usually available on their website and adhere to them religiously.

Basic Word Count Guidelines:

Chapter book (6-8 yr) 5-25,000 words

Middle Reader (8-12) 25-40,000 words

Young Adult (12-18) 40-75,000 words (middle reader and YA kids like to read about characters a couple of years older than they are)

Novelette 7,500–20,000 words

Novella 20-30,000 words, 80-120 pages

Short Contemporary 50,000-60,000 words, 200-240 pages

Long Contemporary 70,000-80,000 words, 280-320 pages

Short Historical /Mainstream 90-100,000 words, 360-400 pages

Romance novel 90-100,000 words, 360-400 pages

Long Historical/ Mainstream 108,000-120,000, 432-480 pages

These are ballpark figures, and the submission guidelines for a particular publisher should be the final word on the matter.

For first time authors, publishers tend to want between 80-100,000 words. A person submitting above what they are looking for should consider that each 10,000 words over the guideline is a ten percent increase in print costs, and publishers are not into paying more money on unproven writers.

CHAPTER SEVEN

LIGHTS . . .
CAMERA . . .
ACTION

*What is the most common reason that
manuscripts are rejected?*

G ood question. In a perfect world it would be all about the writing, but as we have seen in our study of the proposal, a lot of things enter into the decision process before an agent or editor decides the project might be a fit for them and decides to read a full manuscript. The good news is that it comes down to good writing after all.

I don't mean a good book. Those accepting submissions see hundreds of good books and surely can't take them all. They are looking for exceptional books. They're looking for a unique story or subject, well written in a unique voice, one they can see a clear market for.

We've all heard by now — or we should have — that the first page is the big test. We have to force that reader off the first page, make them turn it and commit to reading. Push them down into the chapter, because if we get them to commit, chances are we will get that editor to commit as well. And I don't mean encourage them to turn the page, or hope they will, or interest them. We need to force them to turn the page.

But we're still in the game, we have survived the tests, so now we get worked into the reading schedule. The house has a certain number of slots, and the editor has to pick the best fit he or she can find, go into committee, and try to get that project accepted. If our project is starting to look like a contender, we're probably going to get the opportunity to submit the full manuscript. The last test is to make sure we have maintained good writing and flow all the way through the book.

Eighty to eighty-five percent of manuscripts have been rejected by this point. That's pretty high, but now we see why they were rejected, and on a majority of them it wasn't even an editor's decision. They simply failed a test and chances are it was something the authors themselves did or didn't do. But do you know what the good side of this is? If we do it all right, if we write a good manuscript, do the targeting and do a professional submission, then eighty percent of the manuscripts submitted are no competition at all.

Don't get me wrong, making the twenty percent doesn't guarantee a sale. Remember, we talked about the importance of the puzzle parts being there, even with a wonderful manuscript. There's nothing we can do about that. But we can do something about submitting only to places where we know our works fit in.

Those that are left are in the game. They are a potential fit or they would not be sitting on the desk ready to read. So what can stand in their way now? As I said, the most common thing is that the author fails to get the reader off the first page or fails to hook them into the story within the first dozen pages.

So many writers think they are through when they write the story. Actually, that's when crafting the story begins. Like a director of a movie who takes all the raw scenes that he's shot and starts weaving them into a movie, the writer takes the raw chapters and starts working on the pacing and the flow, engaging the reader here and picking up the pace there. Moving scenes to push a reader at the end of one chapter into the next. Watching to see that it doesn't slow down to a point where the reader loses interest. In my opinion, we then need to take off our writer hat and direct this piece — make it flow so we pull the reader in, then subtly guide them through it.

Like the director in the cutting room, I'm now taking a story that I thought was complete and cutting here and adding there to make it flow. Some things get left on the cutting room floor. I'm not changing the story at all, but I find places where an additional scene must be shot to better transition a dead spot. Places where a camera must be moved to get a different POV. Hitchcock was the master at this and believed the camera must be moved every few minutes to keep the interest of the audience. A lot of writers watch a movie with attention to what the screenwriter has crafted. I like to watch and see what the director has done to make the story flow. This is a major failing with a large percentage of submissions that come in. They have a good story, the writing and editing is good, but the flow is just not there.

In my own writing, my first chapters are not necessarily intended to be permanent. They are simply a means of getting the story moving. After I have finished the first draft, after I know my story and my characters well, then I will go back and write the first chapters. Sometimes I find that what I had written initially does not really fit in the story at all. Sometimes I find the story actually starts in a different place than I thought. It doesn't pay to fall so in love with your first chapters that you can't evaluate them objectively.

The very last thing I do after I am happy with the whole manuscript is to look at that first page and say, "Now, how do I get the editor off this page? How do I get that reader off the first page?" I like to see a question asked that is not answered, an action initiated that is not finished, curiosity aroused but not satisfied, anything that forces them to turn the page and make that mental commitment to read. This is critical when that reader is standing in a bookstore, sampling back cover blurbs and first pages until someone forces them off that first page and down into the book.

How do I hook them into the story in the first dozen pages? Literary fiction has all day to set the scene, introduce the characters, or paint a pretty picture; readers of the genre are prepared to make that time investment. But most commercial fiction readers decide to read or not read within the first dozen pages. How do we hold them? Once we have them off that first page we have to immediately give them a sense of story, draw their interest and keep it.

A substantial number of people feel compelled to draw the scene in great detail so the reader will have a sense of the setting. It is important to acclimate the reader, but most readers don't care much about the setting until they have made the decision to read. Like Hitchcock moving the camera every few minutes to draw the reader into the scene, I believe it is best to spread the setting details and intersperse them with the story to keep driving the reader forward. Large blocks of narrative are to be avoided, particularly in the critical first dozen pages.

I don't know about you, but I tend to wrap up scenes and chapters like little short stories. Great for a short story, but for a chapter? Not so much. With my director hat on I look at how each chapter ends and what I need to do to push the reader on to the next chapter. If a book flows correctly, the reader should not be able to find convenient places to put it down.

The highest compliment I ever got on my work was from one of my wife's clients who was at the hospital awaiting her first grandchild. For some reason she could not be in the delivery room and was reading one of my books as she waited. They called her to come meet her grandchild, and without thinking she put up a hand and said, "Just a minute, I can't stop here!"

I'm sure she quickly came to her senses, but even that brief second was the highest compliment a writer could get.

With the director hat on, we can see the places where the story isn't flowing — dead spots. They have to go. We can see scenes, maybe even scenes that we love, but they just don't move the story forward, they are just "tacked on." Cutting words is like killing our babies, but agents and editors are looking for the things that distinguish a good book from an exceptional book.

We mention the negative eighty-five percent failure-to-connect rate, but the fact is, if an editor or agent reads a manuscript all the way through, he will try to take it. An editor may have to go into committee to fight for the book and try to get it accepted, but if he reads the manuscript all the way through he is likely to want it, even if there are problems with it. Why? Because he doesn't read to finish manuscripts, he reads to find that point where he knows it doesn't work for them. If we force him to keep reading, and he reads all the way through, chances are he will feel confident that a reader will do the same. We didn't give him a convenient place to quit reading or an easy spot to put it down.

That's the secret. We all need to put that director hat on, grab that megaphone, yell, lights...camera...action... and direct that piece.

CHAPTER EIGHT

THE LAST HURDLES

*Let's say the formatting checks out
and we passed the various tests, are
there still things that can go wrong?*

I'm sorry to say, yes.

Is there an SASE in the submission packet if the guidelines call for one? No? How is the editor going to get back to us? They probably won't. Most rejections happen right at this point without reading any of the writing. Wrong genre? Way too short? Way too long? Bad spelling and grammar on the cover letter? Overtly poor fit (like erotica at a Christian house or vice versa)?

Silly stuff can get us rejected, like colored fonts and fancy paper, or photocopies so faint the editor can't read them. Again, this is not the place to stand out. You want your submission to look just like the ones being sent in by experienced professional writers. Editors are not under any obligation to like, or for that matter, to even read our stuff. It's our job to make it easy on them and to compel them to like our writing.

Is it unique, or have they published something similar recently? If they have, there's nothing we can do about that. With the obvious stuff gone the editor will probably look over the proposal's table of contents to see if all of the requested items are there. No synopsis? How are they supposed to see the story line to determine if they want more? A twenty pager? It's a synopsis, not a *Reader's Digest Condensed Book*. Some will read the synopsis right off, others don't want to read it at all unless the writing really speaks to them. Holding back the ending to intrigue them? It won't. They'll probably just toss it.

  Another topic that is pertinent to this discussion is the role of agents in this endeavor. Many of the publications note they want agented proposals. A good many agent websites mention they aren't taking new writers or they want a recommendation from one of their existing writers. Can you share any wisdom on the need or benefit of obtaining an agent during the marketing of a book proposal process?

You're right, that is pretty much a topic all by itself, but I'll hit the high spots.

Do we need an agent to get published? No. I mentioned earlier that the majority of writers published before they got an agent. In a survey I did a few years ago, that number came in above eighty percent. (It amazes me how often that eighty percent number shows up.) This is why I encourage writers to query both publishers and agents. However, having said that, most listings in the market guide say "agent only" or "meet the editor at a conference." While it is possible to get into a larger house unagented, the odds are slim. Chances are, all we are accomplishing is burning a bridge on which an agent could have made a successful submission.

The houses which authors query are the small and some mid-list houses that say in their submission guidelines that they will accept unsolicited submissions. Most writers start at small houses; very few hit a major contract out of the park with a big publisher first time at bat. It has to do with having realistic expectations. And yes, most agents and editors are looking for people with some publishing credentials and a great platform.

We can afford to have just so many writers in our clientele at any given time who are brand new and have neither. I don't gamble, but I understand statistics and playing the odds well enough to know if someone goes to the race track and bets nothing but long-shots he won't win very often. For an editor or agent to have the luxury of trying to help some newcomers break in, they had better have a solid base of clients who are very saleable, giving them the ability to try and help those long-shots, or they won't be in business long enough to get it done.

And there are some people who just don't need an agent. I have a number of writer friends who have always done their own thing, have good contacts, and negotiate a pretty good contract. Why would they give me fifteen percent of the deal? Just because I'm such a great guy? I don't think so. There are also some people who don't need a publisher either, all they need is a printer. If we need a book only to complement our speaking or workshop, and we realize there will probably be little sales outside of that, why let the publisher, the agent, and the bookstores make most of the money? I did a little Chamber of Commerce directory covering those who had served managing chambers over the years. I knew exactly who the market was, and I was the one who would sell it to them if it got sold. I went to a plain printer and had 5000 books printed and sold them to the people who made up that market. Involving other people would have been just giving money away.

But for most writers, having an agent gives them a foot in some doors otherwise not open to them, expertise with contract negotiations, a knowledge of what publishing opportunities are in an industry that literally changes daily. Agents give us advice and assistance, an advocate to work with publishers on our behalf. Usually an agent will affect the process enough that they earn their keep.

   Can you explain more on this comment? "While it is possible to get into a larger house unagented the odds are slim. Chances are, all we are accomplishing is burning a bridge on which an agent could have made a successful submission."

Sure, if they say "agent only" and we submit to them anyway, chances are we are going to be rejected. Agents and editors keep records, and if later the author should get an agent who tries to submit it, those publishers are just going to say they have already rejected it. That bridge is burned. That's why we ask for the history of the manuscript in our proposals. In other words, who has seen it? If it seems to be a pretty good book but everybody and their dog has already seen it, who are we going to sell it to? An editor won't look at it again simply because it is an agent sending it to them, and it is embarrassing for me to send one that they have already rejected. That usually occurs when someone has not been forthright in telling me where the manuscript has been submitted. If we take a book back to a publisher who has seen it before, it is only because it has been rewritten and reworked and is an altogether different submission. Even then I make sure they know it is a resubmission. And I don't just send it, but ask for permission to send it again.

> ℒ *In a past issue of* Poets and Writers, *there is an interview with five agents. Some of what they say is discouraging (most of it actually). First, they said they don't even read the synopses, but skip over them to the first page because they think they're terrible. Ugh! Is this how it is for every agent? We writers hate writing them, then after going to the trouble, they don't read them. Second, there are only about 100 people in the United States who make their living off novel writing. Third, one agent states, "For 99 percent of people writing fiction [getting published] shouldn't necessarily be the goal." Another states, "I think being published has come to feel too achievable." What do you think of this?*

There is a lot of truth here. I just stated it a little gentler. I said that agents and editors are going to personally handle one or two thousand submissions in a year. They know going in that they can only select a handful, therefore most will be rejected. They know that. I know that. Eighty to eighty-five percent were never going to be substantially published. They just aren't willing to do the things they need to do, learn the things they need to learn to make their book the caliber it needs to be. They aren't going to be willing to perform the business side we have been talking about, work on the synopsis, the proposal and the marketing information, and have a good platform and marketing plan.

I also said right up front that "getting published is not a selection process but a survival process." People looking at our project plan to reject it. They are going to reject most of them, so why should we be any different? Our job is to survive all of these rejection points and still be sitting on the desk after they have worked the pile. Our job is to get into the fifteen to twenty percent that have jumped through all of the hoops and are really going to be considered. Then it is all about the writing competing for a few slots, and the best writing in that person's opinion wins. We will normally know if we are in the fifteen to twenty percent when a full manuscript is requested.

I have no problem being beaten out by someone who had a better crafted story as long as I am in that final percentage and haven't blown it on some stuff that was my fault. I want it to be about the writing.

As to publishing being more achievable, there are a huge number of companies pandering to get our book in print. Some of them will be very expensive, some not too bad, and they will even give us the ability to have our book listed with a major distributor so it can be placed into bookstores. That "can be" is the operative phrase. They don't have a sales force and will not be out selling it into any bookstores, so the sales burden is on the author. For someone who is going to be speaking at workshops all over and needs a book to sell at them, this can be a great option. For someone who is doing this because they can't jump through the hoops necessary to become traditionally published, the number of hoops necessary to sell a self-published book are much greater. The average self-published or POD book sells less than a hundred copies, and nobody but the printer makes any money. I don't say anything at all against self-publishing—I have a couple self-published books myself—but I guarantee I know what is involved, what I am likely to get, and I didn't go into it blind. The majority of my books are traditionally published.

❦ The editing/publishing/agent world is very fickle — opinionated. No matter how much research we do or whoever reads it — what it comes down to is being in the right place at the right time with the right product.

Exactly, right place/time/product. But I don't think "opinionated" puts the right spin on it. Agents only get to select a handful of books out of what is presented to us so we have to select what we really connect with. Not that others we have passed on are not good, but we can only represent projects we really like, really believe in, and feel like we have the right contacts with whom to sell them. We all have different tastes and read books which others like but we don't, and vice versa. It's the same for an editor, they have to pick projects they are willing to go into committee and fight for to try to capture one of those open slots.

I had a professor teaching a course one time who told me something about communicating with people that has really stuck with me. He said to pretend I had a box of index cards, and on those cards is written the sum total of my family values, my education, my experience, everything that has happened to me and everything I have learned. When I want to communicate with someone, I go through my box and, using these cards, I compose what I want to say. But then comes the kicker. When they get my message, they open their box, and all the cards are different; but they have to use their cards to decipher my message. This happens constantly in all of our activities, and it happens with our manuscripts. We use our box of cards to write our story, but that editor or agent will read it using their box of cards . . . as will the readers. It explains why things bounce differently off different people.

⟨♫⟩ *This also explains why a manuscript is rejected by several agents, but later becomes a best seller. It seems too often that no one really knows what good writing is — they only know what it "ain't."*

Excellent comment—and let me tip-toe very carefully through this. We do need to learn to be very discerning about input we receive. Back when I first started writing, I began soaking up everything I could learn to the extent that I knew it backwards and forwards. I could parrot it with the best of them. I even became an officer in the local writing group and became a dispenser of such knowledge. Then I made a couple of well-published writing friends, and when I tried my large store of knowledge on them I got shot down, actually laughed at.

One of them told me I was the "blind leading the blind." I had been passing on the same sort of bull that all of us unpublished people had been trading amongst ourselves as truth. I stunned the writing group by apologizing to them, and I said I would not teach any further courses until I had reason to believe what I was passing on was solid as far as I knew. That is to say, I often give the disclaimer that other people will see things differently than I do, and I have no problem with that. But if I have fifty people passing on what seems to be the current wisdom, and one well-published writer or industry professional telling me something else, it is pretty clear who I should listen to.

I believe what I have passed on in this course is the truth as my background has provided it to me. Is it the only truth? No. And in your statement you are exactly right. If we survive our way into that top fifteen to twenty percent, then it ultimately becomes how well the manuscript we are pitching connects with the person we are pitching it to. Plain old personal preference. It's possible for me to get a good book and just not connect with it (particularly if I just don't see a place for it in the current markets that I'm trying to satisfy). That says nothing about the quality; it is just about the fit.

CHAPTER NINE

HAVING REALISTIC EXPECTATIONS

*The bottom line is this: most successful
authors are those who simply refuse
to give up.*

Rejection slips, the nemesis of all writers. The secret to not letting them get to us is to have realistic expectations when we begin to query. Publishing is a numbers game. It's a matter of being in the right place at the right time with the right product. That's a lot of variables, and they are not going to all line up very often.

My favorite illustration of this is from the old 1960s TV show, *Laugh In*. At the end of the show, the cast in turn started throwing open a window and delivering a line, then somebody else opened a window and answered them. That's the publishing industry. At any given point in time our project may fit in only one place in the whole publishing industry. A short time later it may fit in only one other place in the industry. Our job is to get that manuscript in there while that window is open.

Too young to remember *Laugh In*? Ever gone to the arcade and tried to hit the gophers with the rubber hammer? Same concept.

Remember that experienced writers are going to skim the cream off the top, capturing those open publishing slots, since they are a known quantity for the publisher and have an established fan base. Proven sales.

Remember also that eighty percent of the submissions are not formatted correctly or fail in some of the writing basics, so they get tossed without any fanfare or consideration.

Realize that it takes time; we have to knock on a lot of wrong doors to find the right one. But we can improve our odds with correct writing and formatting, and with good networking and market research so that we are querying where we have a decent chance of success.

The bottom line is this: most successful authors are those who simply refuse to give up.

CHAPTER TEN

FOR CHRISTIAN AUTHORS

If a Christian writer sold only one copy [of his book],
but it changed someone's life,
he would be a success.

At the Heart of America conference in Kansas City, I had to change much of the content of my keynote address at the last moment. After I did, a number of people came up and said the speech touched an urgent need. At another conference, I found myself taking my "Using Fiction to Spread God's Word" workshop in a new direction that I had neither planned nor decided in advance to do. It just happened. Again, I had a couple of people come up and say it had addressed an urgent need.

I said, "So you're the one God changed my talk for."

God does that. It has happened over and over.

There are two ways to write for the Lord: to be called to do it or to decide to do it (in which case it is not a calling but an offering). I don't believe that everyone who would like to write for the Lord has been called to do so any more than I believe that everyone who would like to preach has been called to do so.

How do we discern a calling and know what the Lord wants us to do?

This is intensely personal and not something one person can decide for another, but there is a way someone can help describe the process. If God calls us to do something, He usually isn't subtle about it. If He tells us to do something, it is generally verified several different ways. We may start noticing a common thread in sermons at church, in our Bible reading, in Sunday School, in exchanges with family and friends. If the calling is genuine, as long as we are undecided, the affirmations will continue until we "get it."

Hearing this brought relief to a couple of people who were distressed because they had not heard this calling and felt bad when they'd heard people say they should have. They didn't hear it because they weren't called, but there is absolutely nothing wrong with dedicating your writing as an offering to God. If it is done right, it will be well received and the effort blessed.

Then a couple of people were distressed about how long the process takes and thought surely everything would happen quicker if God had called them to be writers. I pointed out how long God prepared Moses and Abraham and the Apostles, and even Jesus Himself before God began to use them for what He had called them to do. If God has called a writer to a task, He will prepare them before He brings the task to fruition. I stressed that He would not only ensure that the writing was what He wanted it to be, but that the writer himself was where He wanted him to be as well. It is even possible that instead of going faster with God's help, it might take longer than it would for a person preparing an offering out of his own abilities and resources. It most assuredly will take longer if the person is not submitting himself to Him and to the way He wants it done, because success is not likely to come until that happens.

Christian authors not only need to determine whether their writing is a calling or an offering, they need to determine who they are writing for. It makes a difference whether we are writing for the body of believers, or whether we are writing with hopes to plant a seed with a non-believer. It is possible to do both at once, but as in so many things, trying to do such a diverse task with a single book means neither will be done as well as if it were solely focused on a single task.

The big difference between the two is how early any faith content might show up in the book. In a book written for believers, it shows up early and often, giving encouragement and spiritual nourishment. For a non-believer, faith content should not show up until after the reader has become invested in the story and is not likely to put it down. Not that we are trying to fool anybody; we just want to give the message a chance.

You see, faith content, if read and understood, has the effect of putting the reader under conviction by the Holy Spirit. It's how it works. Being under conviction is never comfortable even for believers who understand what it is and why it is gnawing at them. But for someone who does not have the faith to understand what is going on, it can be like wearing a hair shirt. Unless they are fully invested in the story and want to know how it is going to play out, they are quite likely to put the book down.

Quoting scripture at them can also put them off. There aren't that many people who can quote scripture verbatim and give the chapter and verse. Most of us paraphrase, "You know, over in the Book of John it says something about . . ." That sounds normal, the way we would likely say it in conversation. The only time I quote chapter and verse is if the character is actually reading it.

Never focus the faith content directly on the non-believing reader. Talk about making them uncomfortable! They should never be aware that we are talking about our faith. Instead, we have characters who have faith and characters who don't, and our message is carried in the interaction between them. This is not threatening. Non-believers aren't being preached at, they are watching the interaction between the people in the book. But they are smart enough to draw the conclusions about how it affects them.

Finally, as Christian authors we have to know and be content with our role. There are those who sow the seeds, those who nourish and fertilize the crop, then those who get to reap the harvest. It is rare that anyone would ever find their way to the Lord just from reading a book.

Most of the time the role of the author is simply to sow the seed. Maybe on a more advanced level they get to produce material that might be helpful in the nourishing and fertilizing of the crop. But it usually takes personal contact to reap the harvest, something very difficult for a book to do.

But the role of sowing the seed is so important. Without it the others in the process can't do their work at all. Then periodically we discover that our work really is affecting someone's life It doesn't take much of that kind of feedback to make it all worthwhile.

A secular writer has to sell thousands of books to be a success. If a Christian writer sold only one copy, but it changed someone's life, he would be a success.Not that we don't want to reach as many people as possible with our words—we do. But our measurement of success is different.

CHAPTER ELEVEN

WORKING WITH AGENTS AND EDITORS

Miscellaneous Final Thoughts
SOME DO'S AND DON'TS

Don't send out mass mailings to agents or editors addressed "To whom it may concern" or something equally innocuous. As I said earlier, we might as well write "Dear Occupant" on the letter. It is even worse if the email submission actually shows the distribution list of all of the others it is being sent to.

In actuality, a majority of these are thrown away or deleted. If an author does not take the time to make the submission a personal correspondence, then it doesn't deserve a personal response. If it is a hard copy mailing, it is a waste of postage. I know it takes a lot of time to check the submission guidelines for each agency and to insure we are sending what they want the way they wish to receive it — time we could be spending writing — but it is an even bigger waste of time to not do it right and to miss an opportunity that might have been there had we submitted properly.

Don't claim we have a relationship when we don't, or claim publishing credits or sales that are not true. Claiming someone recommended us when they didn't is even worse. Having a truthful relationship with an agent or editor is so important. I don't want clients to not trust me or have faith in me, and I should be able to trust them too.

Do wait until your manuscript is as flawless as you can make it. We need to submit our best work, not count on connecting with an agent or editor who will help us polish it for submission. Not that the polishing is not going to happen, but first the project has to be accepted, and we are all up against a ton of people trying for few agent and publishing slots, and most of them are sending their very best.

Don't copyright your book yourself; that's the publisher's job.

From a legal standpoint, your book is considered copyrighted from the time you finish writing it. Also, the book will more than likely change significantly in form from the time when you received the copyright to the time it is actually in print. And having a copyright on the book shows an agent or editor how long you have been shopping the book around.

Don't send an email that is blank and simply attach the proposal. We don't open emails that have attachments and nothing in the email to tell us what they are. The best thing is to copy the cover letter into the body of the email but leave it in the proposal as well.

Don't just tell me where your proposal is located online. You will find that most editors and agents will not go browsing online to see what you have. We expect a good professional proposal, one on which we can build a strong agency proposal.

Do send attachments in Microsoft Word or as an .rtf file so we can open them. We can open a .pdf file but don't like to get them as we can do nothing but look at them.

Do show up front in a submission what the word count and the genre are so the agents and editors can adjust their thinking.

Do your market analysis. Agents and editors want to see comparables that are not too large (grandiose claims) or too small (why bother?); comparables that will give them a frame of reference for who the readers are.

Do be open to revision ideas and critique without getting your back up. The object is to get the best book possible, not just for the editor to throw his weight around.

Never send back an obnoxious reply to a rejection. Why would we want to burn a bridge that we might try crossing again in the future? These notes are entered into the logs of the submissions, and logs are forever (which explains how we know when you submit a project to us again a couple of years later). Quite the opposite, a brief note thanking the agent or editor for their time is appreciated.

FINAL QUESTIONS

∾ *I have this great personal experience story . . .*

Actually, the market for personal experience stories depends on who knows you and wants to read your story. If the answer is that you are not well known, then that pretty much defines the potential market for a publisher. I often suggest to people who are unknown but have a pretty good story to rewrite it as fiction. Most writers are drawing heavily on their own personal experiences to write anyway, and if there are places in the story that could stand to be "punched up" a little, well, it's fiction. Make it read the way you wish it had gone.

Nonfiction in general is changing. It is harder to sell just on proposal anymore, particularly for a new writer. The subject needs to be something that cannot be found readily online for free in a search, and the publisher likes to know that the author is the one person who can write the book. The visibility and platform for helping sell the book may be even more important than the content of the book itself.

∾ *Should I have a website and participate in social networking before I have a book to sell?*

Of course. First, if we wait until after we have a book out, who do we have to announce it to? Before it comes out we try to establish as many relationships as possible because those relationships are where all that positive "buzz" comes from which helps drive the initial launch of the book. But more important, that is part of the platform so crucial to agents and editors in evaluating the potential of a project.

∾ *Why do agents attend conferences?*

I can tell you this, it certainly isn't to make money. Even in conferences that cover expenses and pay honorariums, I seldom end up in the black. I go to find that next great project. I go to interface with editors and to shore up my relationships with them, and I go to keep my finger on the pulse of the industry. I also go because one of my special gifts has been identified as the gift of encouragement, and I teach programs and workshops and meet with writers needing that gift.

ᑫᕦᒧ *When is it time to change agents?*

First of all, refer to the chapter on "Realistic Expectations" preceding this section.

A person who hops agents often because things don't go as quickly as they want can find themselves in a position where other agents don't want them. Publishing takes time. But if we reach the point where we don't think the agent has the right contacts for us, perhaps it is time to connect with one who has a set of contacts better suited to us. That's the reason I'll part with a client: I feel I've exhausted my contacts for their work, and that I might be hindering them instead of helping them.

Having said this, I spend a huge amount of time and effort getting some debut authors into print. Most of the time this entails a modest start (which of course probably doesn't even cover my out-of-pocket costs). I do this because I have a heart for helping writers get started, but also I do it hoping my investment in them will pay off once their career gets rolling. Sometimes authors then jump to a bigger agency or better known agent once they have some credentials under their belt. This is infinitely unfair to the agent who invested so much in getting them started. My clients have a right to expect loyalty from me, but I should be able to expect it from them in return.

❧ *Will you automatically take my next book?*
Different agencies may differ on this one. My answer is "not automatically." Our contract, unless it is written for a single project (not common), is for all book length work. We want to grow an author and participate in the development of their career, and plan to do so. However, this should not mean taking a book to represent that we would not take if it were a new submission. That would weaken and cheapen our efforts and hurt not only the client in question, but all clients at the agency. We surely don't want editors groaning when they see another Hartline Submission. We want them smiling and looking forward to reviewing it.

❧ *Is it true that a book of more than 120,000 words will be rejected?*

Yes, it's generally true, but there are exceptions to the rule. If a publishing house is asking for 90-100,000 words, and the manuscript in question is 165,000 words, then every 10,000 words the manuscript is over becomes a ten percent increase in publishing costs. That's not something a publisher wants to do with an unproven author. We gave some broad word count guidelines earlier, and being very far over — or under for that matter — can be a deal breaker.

❧ *Should I have a separate agent for fiction and nonfiction?*

This happens, but I rarely see it work well no matter what the reason. For the most part, it is better to have an agent who has your entire career at heart.

❧ *How much is an advance?*

That's negotiated deal by deal and can range from no advance to six figures. It's money that's advanced against expected royalties and the advance is going to depend on how many books the publisher reasonably expects to sell. For instance, if an author earns a dollar a book and the publisher expects to sell 5000 copies, they'd want to offer a $5,000 advance. Once the author has hit the 5000 copy number they have "earned out" and begin receiving royalties. It's to the author's advantage to earn out, so an advance that they can reasonably reach is in his best interest from a career standpoint.

How much editing is the agent going to do?

It isn't reasonable for agents to give away thousands of dollars worth of editing when they are not likely to be able to recoup that. I make comments on story structure and formatting and flow. Sometimes my editorial assistants do editing on a project before it comes to me. They make recommendations or try to get it to a place that might interest me. But generally, I'm an agent, not an editor. Some other agents may be very hands-on with the editing. Each is different and has different strengths.

How much contact with my agent should I expect?

Well, daily phone calls and hand-holding are pretty much out of the question. I have all of my clients in an online group (which contains a separate room for the ones that want to critique each other's work), and this online group is where I send weekly updates and announcements of sales. The updates and the announcements go to everyone. I find they feel it is encouraging to discover that some in our group are having success even if it is not themselves right at that point in time. Beyond the updates, the group is divided between those who only want the updates and those who want to be able to network with each other. The majority want to network, and they share victories and defeats, pray for one another and encourage one another. I participate in this group discussion. Individual contacts are made to a client the moment a submission is made on their behalf or when a response is received. Periodically, we just talk about where the author is and where he sees his career going.

  What does it mean when an agent shows an AAR designation?

Membership in the Association of Author's Representatives can convey a certain guarantee of credibility. To be accepted into membership, an agent has to agree to not participate in a number of questionable practices as stated in their Canon of Ethics. In addition, the agent has to have a certain amount of achievement in the field.
Yes, I am a member.

  One editor said, "An author isn't my partner until I buy the book, but I'm in business with the agent."

From the agent standpoint, we are hired to represent the interests of the client, but initially it seems to be the opposite. It is our business to know what the editors are looking for and to help them find it. Once a "tentative partnership" is identified we are solely representing the client.
Publishers rely on agents to screen submissions for a variety of reasons. First, it's a cost savings. Cutbacks and the economic situation have made staffing a problem. Editors know that agents go through hundreds of submissions trying to find those products that will be a fit so they don't have to. They know agents are working to stay abreast of trends and of the marketplace and are usually adept at spotting talent. They also know that agents are commissioned salespeople and as such don't just sign anyone, but will spend their time on projects they think have a reasonable chance of success.

*ও I have been offered a publishing contract; do I still need
   an agent?*

Not if you know how to negotiate contracts, avoid publishing
pitfalls, and know what's standard in the industry. Most contracts
are written to the publisher's benefit. If they are hastily signed,
they can leave a lot on the table or have the author giving up
rights they shouldn't, or agreeing to provisions they shouldn't
agree to. In addition, it can be very hard to connect with a good
agent; one of the best times to do it is when you have a contract
in hand to bring to the table.

So, those are a few random q & a's about working with an agent
or editor. I'm sure there are an infinite number more. But just
remember, the bottom line is this: It all starts with writing a
really good book!

ADDENDA

Top ten reasons
I quit reading your submission

TOP 10

10. Generic beginnings: stories that open with the date or the weather or the scenery.

9. Slow beginnings: too much pedestrian detail (characters washing dishes, etc.) or unnecessary background information.

8. Bad grammar, formatting, spelling: writing details that distract from the story.

7. Trying too hard: using big words or flowery prose in an attempt to sound more sophisticated; using big words incorrectly. Awkward or forced imagery is also a turnoff.

6. TMI (Too Much Information): overly detailed description of bodily functions or medical examinations. Stephen King says he doesn't want us to see the cheerleader HE went to school with, but the cheerleader WE went to school with.

5. Clichés: "The buildings were ramrod straight." Or a description, such as a young woman who looks into the mirror and tells us what she sees. Clichés are hard to avoid, but when you revise, go through and try to remove them.

4. Loss of Focus: : no clear narrative; hopping disjointedly from one theme to the next.

3. Head-hopping: jumping from one POV to another without a transition.

2. Unrealistic dialogue or internal narrative.

And the Number One Reason:

Did not force the reader to turn the first page: Not just interest them, but force them. We have one page in which to hook them and drag them deeper into the story, then ten pages to get them invested enough to continue.

SUBMISSION PACKAGE FOR
BEYOND THE SMOKE

SAMPLE COVER LETTER

Date

Name
Address
City, ST Zip code

Subject: Agented submission of Beyond the Smoke by Terry Burns
Thank you for requesting to see this proposal and I enjoyed meeting with you at XXXXXX Conference. Our discussion did indicate that this 50,000 word project might very well be a fit for your current young adult publishing program.

There were no teenagers prior to WWII. Before that time, kids went from what schooling they were going to get to working on the family farm or ranch, or in the city working in stores and factories. Kids don't realize that the things they read about in the Old West, that many of those working the ranches, riding with the cavalry or on trail drives today would be considered teenagers as were most of the riders who were glamorized with the pony express. Girls were very often married by the time they were fifteen. The worst killer in the old west, Billy the Kid, today would be a delinquent teenager. This is the story of two such young people having to grow up fast with all the odds stacked against them.

My agent is Joyce Hart. As an agent in her agency, I have a substantial speaking platform of several significant audiences a month. I have a strong online presence by interfacing with all the major Christian writing groups, with a website that has gone over three million hits, and I am an aggressive marketer and promoter. I would love to send you the full manuscript or discuss the possibility with you.

Blessings,

Terry Burns, agent

ADDENDA

appx. 50,000 words

**Beyond the Smoke
Proposal for a Western Novel**

Terry Burns

Terry Burns, agent
Hartline Literary Agency
xxxx Sunrise Dr #xx
Amarillo TX 79104-4332
terry@hartlineliterary.com
1-xxx-xxx-xxxx
Fax (toll free) 1-xxx-xxx-xxxx

Proposal Table of Contents

Sample Sell Sheet

There were no teenagers before WWII –
young people had to grow up fast . . .
or not grow up at all.

Beyond the Smoke

The west was settled to a large extent by young people. Young men in their teens worked on ranches and served in the cavalry. Young ladies barely in their teens got married and started families. It was a hard land and it demanded young people grow up fast. This is the story of two young people who had to do just that.

Bryan Wheeler is a 16 year old lad who returns from hunting to find the wagon train he is traveling with burned and all of his family and friends dead. His is totally and utterly alone. He walked out a youth and returned to find himself confronted with having to become a man.

He rises to the challenge, but a couple of days later runs across a horrible old man with a girl a year younger than Bryan in his charge. He ends up practically in servitude to the old man himself trying to help her. It is quite a learning experience as they travel together, then one day the old man decides to attack Carol Sue as she bathes in the stream and Bryan, trying to threaten him into stopping, accidentally shoots and kills him. The two young people are now all each other has and everything they encounter seems set against their survival.

Author
Terry W. Burns

Terry has seven novels in print including a three book series from River Oak. He has work in thirteen collections and has four non-fiction titles for a total of 24 books in print. He has a strong platform doing over 20 major events a year as an agent and popular speaker. He has a strong online presence returning at the top of all major search engines with a website that has over 2 million hits with over 250,000 unique visitors. He's a member of the cooperative marketing group, the Christian Author's Network and works with a dozen writing organizations.

Author's Website:
www.terryburns.net

Editor and writer Joan Shoup says: The story is excellent for young adults. The writing is deceptively simple, easy to follow prose, the plot moves at a brisk pace and all strings are neatly tied up in the end. Furthermore, it minimizes romance in the story, instead, bringing out the exciting action--all the while keeping the reader aware that somehow a loving God is present in events and lives. Burns is at his best when he uses his descriptive talents to kernel the Christian message within this tale of the old West.

BEFORE THERE WERE TEENS: SERIES POTENTIAL

Beyond the Smoke

Bryan Wheeler is a sixteen-year-old lad who returns from hunting to find the wagon train he is traveling with burned and all of his family and friends dead. He is totally and utterly alone. He walked out a youth and returned to find himself forced to become a man. He rises to the challenge, but a couple of days later runs across a horrible old man with a girl, CarolSue, who is only a year younger than Bryan in his charge. Bryan ends up practically in servitude to the old man while trying to help her. It is quite a learning experience as they travel together. Then one day, the old man attacks Carol Sue as she bathes in the stream. Bryan, trying to threaten him into stopping, accidentally shoots and kills him. The two young people are now all each other has, and everything they encounter seems set against their survival.

Hounded

At sixteen, Sam Duncan has been doing a man's work since his dad died. When his mom is murdered, he is tried and convicted as her killer. The sheriff thinks Sam was railroaded and lets him escape. The only ones who believe in him are two fifteen-year-old girls who run away from home to help him. Will a legendary Texas Ranger be the end of him or the one to prove his innocence?

Hard Choices

The two boys were just wrestling at a social. Something they'd always done. Jimmy Green didn't intend to kill Bobby Lee Tate, Bobby Lee just hit his head. But back in the mountains, such an accident became a blood feud, and Tate's family wouldn't rest until they had revenge. Jimmy went on the run. He would defend himself, but not at the cost of killing again . . . ever.

Second Chances

Cinderella meets the Old West, complete with a wicked stepmother, a murdered father, and the determined search of a young man out to find the girl and save her. A grandfather determined to get a second chance with the family he let get away from him makes it all happen. A fast-paced story of action and faith.

AUTHOR'S BIO

Young Adult Western Beyond the Smoke from BJU Press was released January 2009, and the first of a three-book YA series he is ghost writing for another publisher is scheduled for upcoming release.

A Promise Kept scheduled from Treble Heart Press in 2009 is a reprint of "To Keep a Promise," a trade paperback and an e-book (one of five finalists for the Eppie Award from the Electronic Publishers Assn) from The Fiction Works. Trade paperback version of "Promise" was nominated for the 2003 Willa award given by the Women Writing the West.

A three-book Mysterious Ways series at River Oak Press led off with a book by the same title in January 2005. Mysterious Ways was nominated for American Christian Fiction Writers' book of the year, and for the 2006 Christy Award. The second in the series titled Brother's Keeper debuted in January 2006, with the third Shepherd's Son released in January 2007. A Russian translation of Mysterious Ways was released, and the book is under consideration for a movie project.

Trail of the Dime Novel is a trade paperback from Eschelon Press and in audio from JBS Publications. Inspirational fiction mainstream Western Don't I Know You? is out as trade paperback from The Fiction Works.

Poetry chapbook Cowboys Don't Read Poetry is available as an eBook and download. Author is included in several short story collections including: two short story collections from the Darkstormy Writers Community, Range Riters anthology published by the Panhandle Professional Writers, a collection From the Heart, Stories of Love and Friendship, from Coastal Villages Press as well as the second volume More stories of Love and Friendship now available, one entitled Living by Faith released by Obadiah Press, and a book of inspirational short stories entitled Soul Matters from Mark Gilroy Communications. Was included in Heartwarming Christmas Stories, from River Oak, in Cup of Comfort for Weddings and in the Inside Writers Guide Series from Topzone.

Over 200 articles, short stories, and poetry published in publications such as two Writer's Digest articles, Roswell Literary Review, The Roundup Magazine, Trailer Life, Meditation Magazine, Texas Highways, Association Management Magazine, Writing for Dollars Magazine, Will Write For Food E-zine, Wee Ones E-zine, Fiction Addiction Magazine, Lubbock Lifestyle Magazine, and The First Line Magazine.

Wrote weekly newspaper columns for the Big Spring Herald, the Pecos Enterprise, the Carlsbad Current-Argus and the Brady Herald for a total of seventeen years. Worked on a project writing biographies of record industry personalities for online catalogs.

Sells books through a number of online sources. His own website has been the number one website in all three categories: western, western author, and inspirational author for some time according to the Alexa site rankings, running over three million hits and over 450,000 unique visitors. Terry does a regular blog on Blogspot.com, on his website, on Bustles and Spurs, and guest blogs on a number of sites.

Terry is a popular workshop speaker, doing several presentations to audiences all over the country each month.

Affiliations: Terry is a member of the American Christian Fiction Writers, was inducted into the Western Writers of America, is a two time president of the Panhandle Professional Writers, and maintains a presence in all the major Christian and many secular writing groups. Terry is a literary agent with Hartline Literary.

MARKETING AND PROMOTION

Author will pursue an aggressive personal marketing and promotion campaign in addition to the efforts of the publisher. Strategies involved include, but are not limited to:

Libraries – book being reviewed by the key reviewers that libraries use to select books to shelve – spoken to groups of librarians – have done some advertising specifically aimed at libraries and have a list of all libraries that I use for direct marketing. Specifically went after school and church libraries as well as public libraries. Get the publisher involved in this as much as possible.

Interviews and Reviews – have done a substantial number of both and continue to schedule both.

Blog Tour – have cultivated a number of blogs and utilized them for a blog tour.

Book Announcement – posted at over seventy online sites – press releases to all of the communities where I have links and connections. Announcement made to those in the database utilizing email as much as possible to hold down costs.

Contest – run a contest with $300 in prizes aimed at reaching out to young people since this is a YA title.

Book Trailer – create a book trailer and post it in nine places.

Home School – BJU press is strong in the home school market – did some advertising aimed at them and went through some online groups comprised of home school parents.

Publicity – articles, guest blogs, short stories in collections, magazine submissions etc. aimed at the chance to say "author of" in the credits at the bottom.

Book Signings and Programs – sales are better at events where I am presenting (had to postpone the book tour because of being laid up with a broken heel but will come back and do the tour as soon as the doctor releases me). Lead and follow up events in community with press releases and interviews.

Direct Mail Sales To Small Bookstores – publisher reps to contact the chains.

MARKET RESEARCH

What makes this book compelling and unique? This is a delightful book that shows young people what their lives might have been like if they had lived in a time Before There Were Teens. Have found no place this specific slant on being a teen has been addressed. The YA market has been a growth area in the ABA for some time and currently is one of the brighter markets in the CBA as well.

Spin off – Can you develop the book into a series or write a sequel? The author already has several completed manuscripts which appeal to the same readership base.

Endorsements – Author can secure endorsements or cover blurb from well known Christian or Western writers if desired including Spur Award winners, NY Times bestsellers and a winner of the National Book Award.

Marketing Analysis – (Comparables)

Louis L'Amour played a role in the development of my work as I have a full set of his books. I believe readers who like him will like mine, and although he didn't write YA, the man still dominates the western fiction rack many years after his death. Other writers that I believe help define the reader base I write for both adult and young adult are:

Stephen A. Bly – Paperback Writer, One Step Over the Border, Adventures on the American Frontier Series, The Dog Who Would Not Smile, Intrigue at Rafter B Ranch. (We've shared the podium on occasion at conferences.)

Sigmond Brouwer – Broken Angel, Nick Barritt Mystery Series, The Angel and the Ring (YA), Accidental Detective Series. (We both contributed to a Christmas collection, "Heartwarming Christmas Stories.")

Al Lacy – Orphan Trains Trilogy, Dreams of Gold Series, Bright are the Stars.

Gilbert Morris – House of Winslow Series, Seven Sleeper Series, Bonnets and Bugles Series, Time Navigators Series.

Catherine Palmer – Prairie Trilogy, also western/ Christian.

Judith Pella & Tracie Peterson – Texas Angel, Westward Chronicles.

BEYOND THE SMOKE

STORY SYNOPSIS

The West was settled to a large extent by young people. Young men in their teens worked on ranches and served in the cavalry. Young ladies barely in their teens got married and started families. It was a hard land and it demanded young people grow up fast. This is the story of two young people who had to do just that.

Bryan Wheeler is a sixteen year old lad who returns from hunting to find the wagon train he is traveling with burned and all of his family and friends dead. He is totally and utterly alone. He walked out a youth and returned to find himself forced to become a man.

He rises to the challenge, but a couple of days later runs across a horrible old man with a girl, Carol Sue, a year younger than Bryan, in his charge. He finds himself practically in servitude to the old man while trying to help her. The two young people end up being all each other has.

The next influence on their lives is a traveling medicine peddler. A highly educated man with wanderlust in his soul, the professor is a profound influence and serves nicely as a chaperone while the love interest develops.

They travel with him to a Cherokee village where Carol Sue meets and learns from a white woman living among the Indians. Since there are a couple of action sequences in the book depicting unfortunate encounters with hostile savages, this scene and another with a young Cherokee boy provide a counterbalance to those events.

The next stop on the professor's route, with the young people in tow, is a ranch where they find a pregnant woman beginning labor. Another learning experience and growth opportunity for Carol Sue and further development of the characters are achieved by this scene.

At long last the trio reaches civilization in a small town. There, in order to protect himself, Bryan turns himself in for shooting the old man. An exciting trial ensues, but he is exonerated, thanks to the oratory of the professor. The youngsters realize they are truly in love and go to the local minister to be married. He decides that they are too young and, in fact, that she should not be traveling with two unrelated males at her age. He gets the court to remove her and sends her to an orphanage until she comes of age.

Bryan is incensed and kidnaps her from the lady who comes to take her to the orphanage. He spirits her away to Texas, with a posse in pursuit. Just across the river entering Texas, they run into their next major influence, a Texas Ranger. He listens to their story, confronts and turns back the posse, and undertakes to deliver the young couple to Clarendon, a town established by Methodist ministers. Here they find comfort and are finally married, after the minister who is to perform the ceremony sees to the conversion of Carol Sue and ascertains himself of their love and good intentions. By this time Bryan is seventeen and Carol Sue sixteen (not uncommon in the west at this time to marry at this age).

The couple had split with the professor in their getaway, him trying to lead the posse away from them, and following their marriage they head via a reverse route to intercept him on his intended itinerary. They run into a band of hostile Plains Indians, and a desperate fight for their life ensues. Just as it appears all is lost, their Ranger friend catches up to them again, and his intervention makes the difference.

Hard times are never far away, though. When Bryan has recuperated, they continue their journey only to run into the posse who has gotten word of where they are and has come to return them for trial and imprisonment. They underestimate Bryan though, and he jumps up behind the sheriff and, holding a gun to his head, disarms them. He holds them captive while

Carol Sue rides to town to bring back their Ranger friend. He comes running. In the interim, they have found the professor was imprisoned for abetting their escape. They arrange a trade, and the Ranger administers a substantial lesson to the so-called lawmen of the posse.

Back together with the professor, they decide to return to Clarendon where they find a wonderful welcome, and expand the professor's medicine business into a thriving enterprise.

Chapter 1

Smoke arose in the distance.

Bryan Wheeler shaded his eyes as he stared at it. Something was not right, but there was no cause for concern.

Not yet.

He headed back that direction, saw tracks and knelt, fingered the tiny tracks, read them as an eastern boy would read a book. A rabbit for the pot.

At sixteen, Bryan was already an accomplished hunter. His frame bordered on husky, solid and well muscled. His sandy blonde hair and green eyes worked with his ready grin to tell everyone at a glance that he was always ready to have fun.

Cowboys his age were common on western ranches as were soldiers riding with the cavalry or the hard, demanding riders of the Pony Express. Girls even younger got married and started families. On the frontier young people grew up fast . . . or they didn't grow up at all.

While his father handled the team or drove the wagon in the Oregon bound wagon train, Bryan was expected to walk out and put meat on the table. It wasn't a new thing. Back in Missouri, he handled this chore while his father worked the fields, beginning when he was barely big enough to keep the muzzle of the big weapon out of the dirt.

His old man would give him a half a dozen bullets and expect an accounting for each and every one; something for the pot, or a reason why a round was wasted. It was the way of the poor farmer. Scarce resources were not squandered.

Bryan stood and went in the direction of the tracks. Unable to see the ground he scanned the tall grass for the tiniest evidence of movement. He moved slowly, bringing his foot down toe-first, Indian style, to minimize noise. Spotting some movement, he took a line to head it off, then waited until the rabbit scurried across a small clearing.

The animal was in the open only a moment . . . but it was enough.

The shot came quick and clean. He scooped it up by the ears and smiled. A nice fat one! It'll make a good stew, he thought.

He shaded his eyes to look off into the distance, wondered where the train was now. He knew it didn't move very fast, but certainly could eat up ground while a guy's attention was elsewhere. He was still puzzled by the smoke on the horizon. It was too early to stop to cook.

He pushed it from his mind again; the wagon boss had probably found a really good campsite and decided to take advantage of it. That meant he had better hurry back with the rabbit, particularly if his mama already had the pot on.

He swung the rabbit in his left hand in order to keep his rifle at the ready in his right. As he moved out, his eyes constantly played across the ground to either side of his path. He wouldn't say no to a little more meat to fatten that stew.

A short time later, Bryan glanced back to check his direction. Hmm, he thought, the fires don't seem to be grouped tightly the way they should be with the train in a circle for the night. They seem to be in a straight line, spread out. That's strange!

He immediately gave up hunting to step out quickly. As the worry came, he put a hand to his chest, a new tightness there. He had difficulty swallowing, his mouth unexpectedly dry.

He reached the top of the rise and his concerns proved to be justified. Bryan caught his breath as he looked down on the train. The smoke wasn't from cook fires, but from the smoldering ruins of burned out wagons. Bodies lay everywhere.

He couldn't help himself; he began to cry. It wasn't the manly thing to do, but he didn't feel very manly right now.

Bryan entered camp warily, rifle at the ready. He tried to not look at the bodies, but couldn't help himself there either. Any other time it would have sickened him, but now it didn't seem real. He moved as if in a dream, his head swimming. The bright splotches of red were everywhere as if splashed by a demented painter. The air was tainted with a sickly sweet smell, but he scarcely noticed it.

He made straight for his parents' wagon, not wanting to see what he'd find there, but knew he had to do it. He had to know. Suddenly he stopped short. There they were . . . dead . . . no one alive in this whole train. He was alone. Bryan sat down hard on a stump, averting his eyes, staring off into space.

He had often been alone before. Alone hunting, alone for a walk, valued time off by himself, but it had always been a temporary thing, an enjoyable respite.

This time he was ALONE! And he didn't know what to do.

More Books From
🚢Port Yonder Press🚢
A ship in the harbor is safe, but that's not what ships are for.
http://portyonderpress.com/

Port Yonder Press is a brand new, small, independent press.
We are a press of no specific genre, but have an enduring love of
the sea and some of our books will reflect that.

What I Learned in Kansas
by Liz Rhodebeck   **Price: $10.00**

Poems by Wisconsin poet Liz Rhodebeck,
and endorsed by Wisconsin Poet Laureate,
Marilyn Taylor.

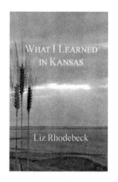

On the Road Home
by Terry Burns   **Price: $12.95**

The first book in The Sagebrush Collection,
On the Road Home contains short stories
and poems about life and love from renowned
inspirational western writer and literary agent
Terry Burns.

Lost Island Smugglers
by Max Elliot Anderson   Price: $12.95

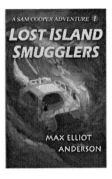

Three friends battle a storm at sea, are stranded on a strange island, and encounter smugglers! Middle-grade readers (and above) will enjoy the new Sam Cooper Adventure Series.

Coming Soon!

The Curse of Captain LaFoote
by Eddie Jones   Price: $12.95

Travel with Ricky Bradshaw through time and space, into a world of pirates, treasure, and adventure, often with comedic results. A Young Adult favorite.

Addenda

9 781935 600039